The Early Chiang Kai-shek:

A STUDY OF HIS PERSONALITY
AND POLITICS, 1887-1924

Occasional Papers
of The East Asian Institute
Columbia University

THE CONTEMPORARY CHINA STUDIES PROGRAM
OF THE EAST ASIAN INSTITUTE,
COLUMBIA UNIVERSITY

The East Asian Institute was established by
Columbia University in 1949 to prepare graduate
students for careers dealing with East Asia and
to aid research and publication on East Asia during the modern period.

Under its aegis the Contemporary China Studies Program was organized in 1959, with the support of the Ford Foundation, for the purpose of
advancing the study of contemporary China. The
program's activities include support of advanced
graduate work, particularly at the doctoral and
post-doctoral level, individual research by
faculty and visiting scholars, research projects,
and the publication of scholarly works on contemporary China.

The Early
Chiang Kai-shek:

A STUDY OF HIS PERSONALITY
AND POLITICS, 1887-1924

Pichon P. Y. Loh

COLUMBIA UNIVERSITY PRESS
New York and London
1971

Copyright © 1971
Columbia University Press

ISBN: 0-231-03596-9

Library of Congress Catalog Card Number
70-158461

The East Asian Institute
Columbia University
New York, N.Y.
Printed in the United States of America

B
C532L

ACKNOWLEDGMENT

Three years ago this month I presented to the
Columbia University Seminar on Modern East Asia:
China a paper on certain aspects of the politics
of Chiang Kai-shek. During the discussion that
followed my presentation, it was suggested that I
undertake a systematic psychological study of
Chiang's politics. Though somewhat skeptical at
the time, I soon came to accept the soundness of
the suggestion. For some time I had indeed felt
that, while Chiang the political man must be as-
sessed, as has often been done, in terms of the
demands of his society, he should be viewed as a
political actor on his own terms as well. Now,
influenced by the discussion, I became persuaded
that whatever bibliographic and methodological
limitations might exist in the study of—and in my
study of—the politics and personality of Chiang,
such an effort would be a step in the right direction. For the invitation to speak to the China
Seminar I thank T.K. Tong, chairman of the seminar
during 1967-68; for the suggestion, Frederick T.C.
Yu, a seminar colleague.

The first draft of the manuscript was completed
during the summer of 1968 and has since undergone
several revisions. In this endeavor, I owe a profound debt of gratitude to C. Martin Wilbur. He
gave me freely of his time, read two of the drafts
with great care, offered insightful criticism on
both broad issues and small details, loaned me his
personal copy of the Mao-Ch'en version of Chiang's
"diary," and otherwise supported and encouraged my
research on Chiang. I also wish to express my
sincere appreciation to A. Doak Barnett, Tang Tsou,
Franklin L. Ho, Thomas L. Robertson, Jr., and Ammon
C. Roth, Jr., all of whom read the entire manuscript at various stages of its development and

v

made substantive or stylistic comments. My thanks
also go to Huang Chi-lu and Howard L. Boorman for
their responses to my inquiries on certain points,
and to Earl H. Pritchard and James T.C. Liu for
their encouragement. For financial support I am
grateful to Upsala College for a Faculty Fellow-
ship in 1967-68 and a subsequent grant from its
Faculty Research Committee, and to the East Asian
Institute of Columbia University for a Research
Associateship in 1967-69. It is a pleasure to ac-
knowledge the administrative officers who have had
a positive part in making these awards and in fa-
cilitating my research: President Carl Fjellman,
former Acting Dean Ralph Hjelm, Dean C. Alfred
Perkins, and Chairman Robert R. Rockwood of the
Department of History and Political Science at
Upsala College; and A. Doak Barnett and the late
John M.H. Lindbeck of the East Asian Institute.

The Chinese characters in this volume were
provided by Loretta Pan. I thank her for her
graciousness. Dale Anderson rendered helpful edi-
torial assistance, and Jeanne Schoch lent her typ-
ing skills to its production. My wife Vivien was
a constant source of inspiration and ever a help-
ing hand.

It goes without saying that I alone am responsible for the data presented and interpretations
given.

Pichon P.Y. Loh
Tenafly, N.J.
February 1971

CONTENTS

The Early Chiang Kai-shek:

A STUDY OF HIS PERSONALITY
AND POLITICS, 1887-1924

I. INTRODUCTION

On April 5, 1925, Chiang Kai-shek returned from the First Eastern Expedition to the Whampoa Military Academy to officiate at a funeral service for Sun Yat-sen, who had died in Peking on March 12. Huang Chi-lu, then a young professor of political science at the University of Kwangtung and destined to become director of the Kuomintang Archives some forty years later, has informed us of the display of strong emotion evidenced by Chiang on this occasion: "The service was officiated by Mr. Chiang and Liao Chung-k'ai and was attended by over four thousand officers, cadets, and soldiers. As the funeral ceremonies began, Mr. Chiang, unable to control himself, wept bitterly and audibly, causing all in the assembly to shed tears."[1] Three years later, at the conclusion of the Northern Expedition, a similarly melodramatic scene unfolded before the eyes of the public as Chiang visited Sun's bier in the suburbs of Peking. Biographer S. I. Hsiung recorded:

> The first thing Chiang Kai-[s]hek did
> when he came to Peking was to perform the
> solemn ceremony of visiting the coffin.
> When he and the three other military lead-
> ers, Feng Yü-[h]siang, Yen Hsi-[shan] and
> Li Tsung-[j]en, made this sacred pilgrimage
> to the West Hill and stood with their un-
> covered heads bowed in front of the coffin,
> Chiang Kai-[s]hek's tears rained down his
> cheeks and soon he broke into uncontrol-
> lable sobs.[2]

These two highly emotional episodes raise several points of human interest and of thematic relevance to the development of the personality

1

and politics of Chiang Kai-shek. First, they contrast interestingly with his quality of stoicism
and tendency toward withdrawal, attributes that
did not go unnoticed by close observers during
his childhood and adolescence and which through
strenuous, even tortuous, self-cultivation were
to become dominant traits in his middle and late
adulthood. Second, the outbursts suggest an unusual experience in ego synthesis--a painful,
emotion-ridden effort to relate to the ever-
expanding world around him, to reach a state of
relative psychological equilibrium between the im-
pulse of his emotions as molded by his childhood
experiences and the compulsion of his conscience
as conditioned by the enveloping societal value-
attitudes. Third, this search for ego synthesis
resulted in a prolonged identity crisis which,
after much wasted effort and confused wandering
through numerous unmarked labyrinths, was finally
consummated in the early 1920s. The essential resolution of the crisis enabled him to find in-
creasing measures of psychological fulfillment in
the Kuomintang and in Kuomintang's China.

These observations suggest that a psychological study of Chiang would be both interesting and
useful: interesting because the complexity of his
personality was presumably reflective of the psychosocial complexity of his times;[3] useful because
an understanding of the personality and politics
of an authoritarian leader who played a critical
role in history can contribute to a further understanding of the character and development of the
political system under his charge.[4] The present
study is an attempt to gain a new perspective on
the politics of Chiang Kai-shek by utilizing his
"diary" and such published material as is cur-
rently available to construct a psychological biography covering his early years. It is thus an

2

exploratory inquiry into the political socialization and recruitment of an emerging authoritarian
leader in terms of his personality as well as the
sociopolitical milieu of his times. It also en-
deavors to establish certain attitudinal regulari-
ties during the early stages of his life, from the
moment of his induction into the family to the
years of his socialization in schools and peer
groups; from the beginning of his identity crisis
in 1906, when he embarked upon a search for a total commitment that would give him meaning in life
as well as psychological equilibrium in his inner
being, to his appointment in 1924 as commandant of
the Whampoa Military Academy, from which he was to
launch a political career as the arbiter and
would-be conscience of the nation.[5]

II. CHILDHOOD EXPERIENCE AND
PERSONALITY FORMATION

In 1887, the biographical sketch of Chiang compiled by his former confidential secretary Ch'en Pu-lei begins, "Chiang was born at 12 o'clock, noon, October 31, on the second floor of the Yutai Salt Store at Chikow, Wuling, Fenghwa [Chekiang province,] and was named Jui-yüan by Grandfather Yu-piao."[6] It is significant—as noted in Chiang's "diary" by his tutor Mao Ssu-ch'eng and in a number of other published works on Chiang—that this family of some local standing claimed descent from the third son of the Duke of Chou and had made its abode in Feng-hua since the T'ang dynasty and at Ch'i-k'ou since the Yüan.[7]

About Chiang's father little is known. According to one adulatory biography, however, he belonged to that branch of the Chiangs which "did not scorn to go into business, especially into the salt trade" and was a second generation salt merchant who sought to rebuild the family fortune after the ruinous Taiping Rebellion.[8] Hollington K. Tong's authorized biography of Chiang, which reads at times more like a historical novel than the novel history it claims to be, has this to say:

Chiang [Kai-shek] was extremely fortunate in the family into which he had the good luck to be born. For generations his forbears had been farmers. His grandfather, who was extremely fond of Chiang, continued the family tradition, but also attained local renown as a scholar. His son (Chiang's father) followed in his footsteps.

4

Stories are still told in Chikow and its environs of the public spirit that was unceasingly shown by Chiang Kai-shek's father--Su-an. If it be true that blessings rest upon the peace-makers, he must have been blessed indeed. When fellow villagers thought of going to law, it became an established practice for them to go to Mr. Chiang to lay the matter before him.[9]

The same account was related by Chiang when he asked his Kuomintang comrade Chu Chih-hsin (Chu Ta-fu) to write an inscription for his father's gravestone in August 1918, twenty-three years after his demise.[10] It is interesting to observe that Chiang wrote personal eulogies for his paternal grandfather, who "always treated and nursed" the frail little boy during his frequent spells of illness,[11] for his maternal grandmother, who "loved my mother and myself with special tenderness," and for his maternal grandfather, whom Chiang had never even seen but whose sterling qualities had been impressed upon Chiang by his mother "since I was a child."[12] Yet, for all the filial piety professed before and since, he could not bring himself to write a personal panegyric for his deceased father.

Chiang's professed relationship with his mother was as warm as the relationship with his father seems to have been frigid. The eulogy he wrote for his mother upon her death in June 1921 is so replete with anecdotes of Chiang's early life and with insights into his thought processes as to be most revealing.[13] In 1886 Chiang's mother, Wang Ts'ai-yü, at the age of 22 (23 sui) was married to his father Su-an, who was 42 (43 sui). She was his

5

third wife, his first having left behind a son
Hsi-hou and a daughter Jui-ch'un, and his second
wife having died without issue. A year after his
marriage to Wang Ts'ai-yü, she bore him a son,
named Jui-yüan, who in later years came to be
known as Chung-cheng and Chieh-shih (Kai-shek by
Cantonese pronunciation). Three other children
followed, daughters Jui-lien and Jui-chü and a son
Jui-ch'ing. Of the three girls, Jui-yüan's sister Jui-chü died young, while his half-sister Jui-
ch'un and sister Jui-lien were married into local
families.[14] His half-brother Hsi-hou, the brain
in the family and "a distinguished scholar" in
the district,[15] completed his legal training in
1908[16] and became an assessor of the Municipal
Court of Canton in 1917.[17] Younger brother Jui-
ch'ing, the darling of the family, was endowed
with "extremely good looks." Jui-yüan, the naughty one, was not known for either his intellect or
good looks.

Chiang's mother found little happiness in her
marriage, if we are to accept Chiang's portrait of
her. Being brought up in a "rich" farming family
from Ko-ch'i in Cheng hsien, Chekiang, she was
"well versed in poetry and other literary subjects
and an expert at needlework"[18] and prior to her
marriage was "well known in her village and neighborhood for her intellect and wisdom." But considering the fact that she was already twenty-two
when married to her busy salt merchant husband
with two growing children to care for, she was
probably appreciated more for her needlework than
for her intellect. "My mother nursed and taught
[Hsi-hou and Jui-ch'un] and brought them up,"
Chiang has told us. Although she was said to have
fostered them "exactly as if they were her own,"
there is reason to believe that she assumed the re-

6

sponsibility as a wifely duty rather than out of
maternal instinct. For Chiang has also asserted
that she "endured thirty-six years of hardship"
from the time she was married in 1886 to the day
she died in 1921, that she "swallowed much bitterness" during the entire period, and that she "never refused any kind of toil." She was, in
Chiang's perception, a virtuous, strong-willed,
humorless, and religious person, duty-oriented and
and very correct.

The birth of Chiang brought her no joy. He
was frequently sick, owing to a frail constitution
as well as to mischievous horseplay:

> In my childhood I was often ill and on
> many occasions the illness was dangerous
> and critical. But as soon as I was re-
> covered, I would play about as gaily as
> ever, hopping and skipping all day long.
> I was, therefore, frequently exposed to
> the risk of being drowned or burnt to
> death, or else severely cut or wounded.
> My poor kind mother's anxiety over me was
> double that of other mothers.

By the time he was five—and "much naughtier than
before"—she apparently had had enough of him and,
upon the counsel of her father-in-law (not of her
husband), committed him to a family tutor sooner
than she had intended.[19] When he was not in the
care of his tutor, she tried, with little or no
assistance from her husband, "to teach and persuade me to study" and, failing that, "to use the
birch repeatedly in order not to spoil me." But
nothing she did seemed to help matters much. More
than anything else, young Chiang was fond of playing war games with the neighborhood children,
appointing himself the commanding general and giv-

ing orders to his playmates. Or he might be found
mounting a platform to amuse a crowd with storytelling, "his manner haughty, his gait lordly, and
his gestures extremely free."[20] Twice during
these five years of "toil" Ts'ai-yü was with child,
and glimmers of hope must have made her life somewhat easier, but the children both turned out to
be girls. These were indeed years of "bitterness"
for her, years during which Chiang seems to have
found neither identification with his father nor
affection from his mother.

Two more years she had to endure before she
found the one genuine solace in her married life:
she had a son, Jui-ch'ing, whom she loved with un-
concealed affection. "Being the youngest of our
generation," Chiang remembered, "and also endowed
with extremely good looks, which none of the
others of us had, he was my mother's favorite."
Chiang also remembered that after his father's
death in 1895, "my mother divided up the estate,
which was allotted to us three male heirs. Because my elder brother was the son of the first
wife, he was given the biggest share." With the
elder brother getting the most money and the younger brother the most affection, Chiang must have
felt a deep sense of alienation. Given this feeling of rejection, Chiang's sensitive ego must have
received a further shock when he, and the entire
village, was told by a traveling fortune-teller
that his cranial structure was quite unlike that
of anyone else and that he was an "exceptionally
strange child."[21] He now found that he had not
only been left out of the family but had become
the laughingstock of the world around him. Growing up in such a perceived environment, it would
be only natural if Chiang was to experience a subconscious desire to seek identification by other
means and to displace his motives onto objects

8

other than those familiar to him during childhood.

   In 1898 Jui-ch'ing, barely four, died.[22]
Chiang was to say twenty years later that his mother's grief over Jui-ch'ing's death was "even
more intense than over my father's demise."[23] According to his eulogy for her, she "mourned bitterly" and, "both mentally and physically, she
suffered intensely. Since then she has centered
all her hopes on me, hoping anxiously that I
should make a name for myself." But the affection
she came to have for the young Chiang, though genuine and lasting, was a poor substitute for the
love she had borne for Jui-ch'ing; that for Jui-
ch'ing came from her tender heart, that for the
"strange" Jui-yüan came from her strong-willed
mind. The bond that developed between the widow
and her fatherless son was thus characterized by
an ambivalent emotional tension that often burst
through the veneer of unsteady calm into uncontrollable passions. Unaccustomed to natural parental love during his formative years, Chiang responded to his mother's forced affection with an
awkwardness and unnaturalness that often assumed
extreme, even contrary, forms. Joy found expression in sorrow; ill-omened dreams marked the
height of filial devotion. Chiang's emotional
tensions were described by Mao Ssu-ch'eng in an
entry in Chiang's "diary" for 1899, the year he
was sent away from home to study with his cousins
at Ko-ch'i:

   During the summer vacation he returned
   home from school. Upon seeing his mother,
   he burst into uncontrollable sobs before
   he could even utter a word, and the cry
   grew more saddening as the wailing went on.
   Thenceforth, the start of each journey never

9

failed to be marked by tear-shedding
until his eyes would turn red, so much
so that the contagion of his grief would
deeply depress the neighbors and cause
his mother to retire to the adjoining
room, there to shed tears herself. After
she had exhorted him and given him encouragement, he would set out on his journey,
weeping for ten or twenty li on the way.
Such were the piteous circumstances between the widowed mother and the fatherless son.[24]

Another adulatory biography tells us that during
his adolescence there were "frequent quarrels between Mr. Chiang and [his] mother."[25]

Chiang's checkered academic career provides
additional eloquent testimony to the unsteady personality that haunted him even in his early adulthood.[26] His schooling began at the age of five
under Jen Chieh-mei. We are told that he was
"playful," "noisy," adventurous, and increasingly
insolent. At the age of seven he had a new teacher, Chiang Chin-fan. At eight he returned to Jen
Chieh-mei, who was now said to be an excessively
hard teacher. Jen died during the summer of that
year (1895) and the boy returned to Chiang Chin-
fan, under whom he was to remain for three and a
half years. According to biographer Hsiung,
Chiang Chin-fan was "a rather stiff scholar" and
"a very painstaking teacher," and the boy made
"slow progress" under him.[27] Tutor Chiang must
also have been a very permissive teacher, however,
for he had high praise for the young boy whose
bluntness, even arrogance, was known to him and
who, at the age of ten, was already entertaining
his mother's guests with the gusto of the Liang-

10

shan bravos. During that year Chiang was introduced to American history, with the American president being presented as an unostentatious figure
and a public servant. It is interesting to note
that while this portrayal evoked amazement in his
status-conscious classmates, it elicited an atten-
tion-getting so-what response from the self-con-
scious Chiang, a fact that must have surprised his
classmates even more. Two years later, at the age
of twelve, Chiang was with tutor Yao Tsung-yüan;
at thirteen, with Mao Feng-mei; and at fourteen,
with Chu Ching-sung. Then during the winter of
1901-02, when he was merely fourteen, he was married to Miss Mao by parental arrangement. After
that milestone in life, Chiang studied under Mao
Ssu-ch'eng, who seems to have known him for a number of years prior to this tutorial relationship.
But Chiang's initiation into "adult" life had little if any effect on his behavioral pattern and
did little to release his inner tensions, as Mao's
interesting diagnosis of his pupil would indicate:

> At play, he would regard the classroom
> as his stage and all his schoolmates as his
> toys: he could be wild and ungovernable.
> But when he was at his desk, reading or
> holding his pen trying to think, then even
> a hundred voices around him could not dis-
> tract him from his concentration. His
> periods of quietude and outburst sometimes
> occurred within a few minutes of each
> other: one would think he had two dif-
> ferent personalities. I was greatly puz-
> zled by him.[28]

If Mao's psychological description is to be
accepted, it may be said that Chiang's personality
structure in his early adulthood had been formed

by 1902 and may be traced to his earlier childhood experiences. We have observed that from the
moment of his birth, Chiang sensed psychological
rejection and learned instinctively to be dis-
trustful of his social environment. As he grew
older and was able to venture outside of his home,
his world image remained unchanged. It was an un-
sympathetic world which in later years he could
not recall with much fondness or gratitude. Furthermore, it was a cruel world that laughed at
the one thing that was his, his physical appearance. But he also learned that he could make himself count in this hostile environment by resort-
ing to extraordinary measures. He found that he
could receive the parental attention he so sorely
missed by creating crisis situations, such as ex-
posing himself "to the risk of being drowned or
burnt to death, or else severely cut or wounded";
and that he could become the center of attention
in class by making outlandish remarks.

At the same time, aided by the gift of fan-
tasy with which all children are endowed by nature,
he developed two equally effective psychological
devices to protect himself against an uncongenial
environment: either he would construct an ideal
world in which he lived in self-sufficiency and
splendid isolation, or he would reduce the uncongenial human beings of the real world to mere
"toys" over which he prevailed in actual (war
games with neighborhood children) or imaginary
supremacy. Not having the opportunity to develop
during childhood a socially acceptable behavioral
pattern of give-and-take and the "normal" habit of
retain-and-reject, he developed instead what may
be loosely termed a crisis personality. He was in-
capable of responding normally and in due proportion to a wide range of emotional situations. But
he could be challenged and fulfilled when confront-

12

ed with a crisis, for under such circumstances he was able not only to summon up the best qualities that were in him, but also to derive maximal psychological satisfaction therefrom. He would feel more "normal" or creative in situations that required leadership and authority, that called for heroic deeds, and that offered suitable opportunities for the projection of his anxieties and suspicions, fear and hostility.

13

III. POLITICAL SOCIALIZATION: EDUCATION
AND EXPLORATION

"Political socialization," explains one study,
"is the process by which political cultures are
maintained and changed. Through the performance
of this function individuals are inducted into the
political culture; their orientations toward political objects are formed. . . . The family unit is
the first socialization structure encountered by
the individual. . . . The school structure is a
second powerful influence in political socialization."29 In the preceding chapter, our emphasis
has been on the personality formation of Chiang as
he was socialized through the agency of the family.
In this and the succeeding chapter we shall be concerned with the processes through which Chiang acquired certain values and attitudes toward his political world, by looking first at the schools and
then at the peer groups that were the agencies of
political socialization in his personality development. In both chapters we shall view Chiang's
induction into the Chinese political culture as
it related to his psychological processes.

Chiang began, as did most pupils in those
days, with the shortest of the Four Books: the
Ta hsüeh (Great Learning) and the Chung yung (Doc-
trine of the Mean), which he finished by the time
he was seven.30 In another year he finished the
Lun yü (Analects) and Meng-tzu (Mencius), thus
completing the Four Books in three years, not a
bad record for an active boy. During this period
he was also introduced to poetry, the Li chi (Record of Rituals) and the Hsiao ching (Classic of
Filial Piety). In 1897 he studied the Ch'un ch'iu
(Spring and Autumn Annals) and T'ang poetry. In
1898 he completed the Shih ching (Classic of Odes),
and in the ensuing year he took up the Shu ching

(Classic of History). In 1900 he read the I ching
(Classic of Changes) and wrote his first poems on
"bamboo" (chu shih); in 1901 he completed the Tso
chuan (Tradition of Tso) and learned to compose
political and general essays. In 1902 he reviewed
the Tso chuan and studied the T'ung-chien kang-mu
(Outline of the Comprehensive Mirror of History)
under tutor Mao Ssu-ch'eng, who recounted Chiang's
first, and last, encounter with the civil service
examination system in the summer of that year:

> He went to the examination to satisfy
> his curiosity and was disgusted by the
> cruel and humiliating regulations of the
> Examination Hall. He severely disparaged
> the Manchu court for the contempt with
> which the young scholars were treated and
> for the despicable habits of decadence and
> pedantry it encouraged, and was greatly
> pleased when he learned, not long after-
> ward, of Yüan Shih-k'ai's memorial to es-
> tablish a new educational system in place
> of the civil service examination.

We may assume that Chiang failed in the examination.

During these years his mother would underpin
his formal learning by giving him personal instruction on ceremonies and sacrificial rituals.
"In rising and sitting, bowing and kneeling, make
certain that the movements are in harmony with the
music of the occasion. Never forget this, my
son." She also required him to read Chang Chih-
tung's popular tract Ch'üan-hsüeh p'ien (Exhortation to Study) after its publication in 1898.

In 1903-04 Chiang studied at the Phoenix Mountain School (Feng-lu hsüeh-t'ang) at the district
seat of Feng-hua hsien, where he received a smat-

15

tering of modern education in English and arith-
metic. But the curriculum was of course heavily
traditional and Chiang remembered receiving instruction in history, the Li chi, and the Chou li
(Rituals of Chou). During his second year there
Chiang, known to his fellow students as the "red-
faced general," led a student protest "in great ex-
citement and agitation" for the alleged purpose of
improving academic matters and was nearly expelled
from the school for having acted in violation of
the general convention, to which he was to subscribe in later years, that the business of students was to study. Chiang soon left the school
of his own accord, transferring in 1905 to the
Golden Arrow School (Chien-chin hsüeh-t'ang) in
Ningpo to study under Ku Ch'ing-lien.[31] Ku, who
delivered the regular lectures on the Classics,
favored Chiang with special assignments: the works
of the ancient philosophers, which introduced him,
among other things, to the legalist concept of political rule; the Shuo wen (Explanation of Writing), a dictionary of over 9000 characters compiled
about A.D.100; the writings of Tseng Kuo-fan,
whose reformist traditionalism and attention to
character building were to have a profound influence on Chiang; and the Sun-tzu ping-fa (Art of
War by Sun Tzu), Chiang's first acquaintance with
military science, which was later to be reflected
in his politico-military policies of divide-and-
rule and of the use of intelligence agents. Ku,
reportedly, also talked of Sun Yat-sen and advised
Chiang to broaden his perspective: "A youth desirous of great achievements must acquire new knowledge. The best way is to go abroad and study in
foreign countries." The advice, if indeed given,
was well received, for the restless Chiang by the
age of eighteen had become so disgusted with local
officials and his kinfolk alike that the idea of a

16

journey abroad, in the name of revolution and new knowledge, must have had a salutary psychological appeal to him.[32]

Thus, at the next school he attended, the Dragon River Middle School (Lung-chin chung-hsüeh-t'ang), Chiang stayed for less than three months, from February to April 1906. Hollington K. Tong, who was a teacher there with a room on the same floor of the school building as Chiang, retained the following "deep impression":

> Chiang Kai-shek was an early riser, and, after his matutinal ablutions, it was his custom to stand erect on the veranda in front of his bedroom for half an hour. During this time his lips were compressed, his features were set in determination, and he stood with his arms firmly folded.[33]

The product of this mental concentration was a resolve to find himself and to relate himself meaningfully to the outer world, in short, to establish his ego identity.[34] His first acts in this quest for identity were typically rebellious — typical of himself and to some degree of his time. Defiantly, he cut off his queue and had it sent home, to the distress and consternation of the entire village. Then, with singleness of purpose and his fare provided by his reluctant mother, he set sail for Japan in May to prepare himself for a military career.[35] Chiang was to recall:

> [In my youth I was naughty and dull-witted and would not subject myself to rules and regulations. And also, because of my humble origin, I was frequently discriminated against and rejected.] Having reached

17

manhood, I determined to go abroad for a
military education. At first many of our
kinsmen and neighbors were quite surprised
at, and some of them were hostile to, my
decision. They certainly would have pre-
vented me from carrying out my wish had it
not been for my mother's resolute will and
her efforts to supply me with the necessary
funds.[36]

In retrospect, two observations may be made
concerning Chiang's sojourns in Japan between the
time of his first journey in May 1906 and his return to Shanghai in late October 1911. First, in
the wake of Japan's soul-stirring victory over
European Russia, Chiang had, like many other restive young men of his time, decided to seek a more
modern education in the most modern nation in
Asia[37] and, as was then quite fashionable, to embark upon a military career.[38] Upon his arrival
in Japan, however, he discovered that without the
endorsement of the Board of War in Peking he could
not matriculate in any of the military academies.[39]
He returned to China half a year later and, with
a stubbornness now characteristic of him, entered
the Short-term National Army School (T'ung-kuo lu-
chün su-ch'eng hsüeh-t'ang, later to become the
influential Paoting Military Academy) in Hopei province in 1907,[40] after having successfully completed a competitive examination to qualify as one of
the fourteen persons selected by merit from Chekiang (forty-six others were selected by nomination, the total quota for Chekiang being sixty).[41]
In early 1908 the Board of War held an examination for qualified cadets from the school for the
purpose of sending the successful candidates to
Japan for further training. Chiang was not among
those considered qualified to sit for the examina-

tion, as he had not enrolled in the Japanese language class. He petitioned the principal of the school, basing his request on the ground that he had studied the language during his stay in Japan. The night before the examination was held, Chiang was "awakened from his dreams" to be informed of the favorable action taken on his petition. He took the examination the next day, passed it, and was sent in the spring to attend the Shimbu Gakkō in Tokyo for a term of three years. In late 1910 he was graduated from the school at the age of twenty-three and assigned to the 13th Field Artillery (Takada) Regiment of the Japanese Army, there to complete his formal military training during the last year of the Manchu dynasty.[42] The dreams he had had in 1905-06 of exploring a new world as differentiated from the old world of limited opportunities in his home district, and of becoming a new, military man unlike the effete scholars he had met in the examination hall in 1902 were realized, through determination and good fortune, by the time the republican revolution erupted.

The second observation to be made about Chiang's study in Japan subsequent upon his "wandering in the wilderness" in 1906[43] is that it resulted in the linking up of his military career with the political leadership of Ch'en Ch'i-mei and, through him, with the revolutionary movement of the Kuomintang. It was in Tokyo in 1906 that he made Ch'en's acquaintance.[44] After his return to Tokyo in early 1908, now as a government-sponsored student at the Shimbu Gakkō, Chiang is said to have been recommended by Ch'en for membership in the T'ung-meng-hui.[45] Despite accounts of later years, it is difficult to tell how close the two men were at this time; but it is known that Ch'en left Japan soon after in the spring.[46] Nor is it possible to verify the allegation that Ch'en in-

19

troduced Chiang to Sun Yat-sen, although it would
be reasonable to assume that such a meeting, if
it indeed took place, would hardly have failed to
be mentioned in the "diary."[47]

It can be accepted as true, however, that
Chiang became interested in and emotionally involved with the revolutionary movement. In 1908,
we are told, he "devoured" the popular revolutionary tract by Tsou Jung, Ke-ming chün (The Revolutionary Army), and thereafter would converse with
the young martyr in his dreams.[48] The "diary"
further informs us that each Sunday Chiang would
call together a number of comrades, mostly from
Chekiang and Kiangsu provinces, for a secret meeting "to deliberate and make plans for important
matters of the revolution." At these meetings
Chiang's expositions on the exploitation of China
by the Manchus and the Powers, reminiscent of the
storytelling of his childhood years, were so gra-
phic and urgent that they "never failed to make
his listeners' hair stand on end." But with the
exceptions of his returns to China during the summers to visit his mother and help "rescue imprisoned comrades"[49] and of the single assassination
attempt he claimed to have made in collaboration
with Ch'en Ch'i-mei during the summer of 1911,[50]
he did not himself assume an active role in the
abortive uprisings that occurred between the time
he joined the party and the Double Tenth at Wuhan
because, we are informed, the party considered the
young cadet to be more valuable to the revolutionary movement at a later and more critical time.[51]

In summary, it may be suggested that during
the nineteen years from 1892 to 1911, Chiang acquired, through the socialization agency of the
school, certain value-attitudes toward the world
of politics. This experience in attitude forma-

20

tion was developmentally related to the earlier experience in personality formation.

Before Chiang's first journey to Japan in 1906, his education was heavily traditional. Although unconventional and sometimes erratic in his behavior, he was nonetheless able to retain something of the traditional education—not enough to pass the civil service examination perhaps, but enough to cultivate in him an abiding faith in the glory of China and also to serve in later years as the foundation of the traditionally oriented value system of the New Life Movement. Among the traditional virtues to which Chiang came to attach the greatest importance was that of li (decorum, propriety, a regulated attitude), a value mediated through his mother and the school system and one that informed his latent personality structure with a propensity for order and a respect for just authority. Thus, at school he would have recurring moments of quietude, attested to by his tutor Mao Ssu-ch'eng, at which time he seemed to withdraw into his ideal world-construct. Similarly, while at the Dragon River Middle School he would spend a half-hour every morning in ritualistic concentration, "with his arms firmly folded," his lips "compressed," and his thoughts apparently turned to a regulated and purposive life situation. Soon thereafter he made up his mind to join the modern army, the institution in transitional China that held the greatest promise for a structured life, authoritatively regulated.

During the impressionable years away from home, Chiang also learned something of the modern world, not enough to make him more than a reform traditionalist in a rapidly evolving transitional society, but enough to give him pride in being an anti-Manchu revolutionary. Restless soul that he

21

was, rebellion against unjust authority was in his
blood. During his childhood and adolescence he
was "naughty" and "would not subject" himself to
rules and regulations imposed upon him by oppressive parental or school authorities. He, the
"red-faced general," was the natural leader of a
student demonstration against poor teaching and a
mediocre curriculum. After his failure in the
civil service examination in 1902 the idea of rebellion against the Manchu dynasty seemed to have
a particular appeal to him. It is not surprising
that his psychological commitment to the alien regime continued to erode thereafter and that he became increasingly susceptible to new patterns of
political behavior. During his stay in Japan, it
was only natural that he should gravitate to those
groups and organizations known for their disen-
chantment with the existing state of affairs, re-
belliousness against the decrepit Manchu regime,
and an activist commitment to the structuring of
an authoritative social order.

It is apparent, then, that Chiang's association with the Chinese revolutionary movement in
Japan was motivated at least as much by the psychological satisfaction he was able to derive
therefrom as by any ideological commitment he had
at the time. Soon after he landed in Japan in
1906, he came to know such activists as Ch'en Ch'i-
mei. What they had in common was not merely a belief in the republican cause, but equally a style
of life, a way of looking at the world of politics, a need to vent long-suppressed psychic ener-
gies, and a tendency to displace private motives
upon public objects.[52] Indeed, Chiang did not read
the popular Revolutionary Army until 1908, five
years after its publication. After having "devoured" it, he put it to good use by surrounding
himself with emotionally dissatisfied overseas

Chinese students and by engaging in wide-ranging
discussions of a highly emotional nature, in which
he would often be the principal agitator. It is
not too much to say, therefore, that after the
turn of the century Chiang was psychologically
disposed to joining the revolutionary ranks and
came to find psychological fulfillment in and
through his association with the T'ung-meng-hui
and its successor, the Kuomintang.

23

IV. POLITICS, IDEOLOGY, AND PERSONALITY,
    1911-1921

A striking feature of Chiang's record during
the decade from the birth of the republic in 1911
to the death of his mother in 1921 is the paucity
of information concerning him. T'ang Leang-li, a
reorganizationist and a partisan of Wang Ching-
wei, provided in 1930 one of the few accounts concerning Chiang's politics and personality, as follows:

> He hurried back to Shanghai [in 1911],
> and was at once commissioned by Ch'en Ch'i-
> mei, the revolutionary Tutuh of Shanghai,
> who was also a Chekiangese, to command the
> 83rd Brigade, a band of some 3,000 men re-
> cruited from the riff-raff of Shanghai. He
> gave his band a severe training, but soon
> he abandoned himself to a life of intense
> dissipation. He would disappear for months
> from headquarters in the houses of sing-
> song girls, and for some reason or other he
> acquired a fiery, uncompromising temper
> which weighed very tryingly on his friends.
> It was during this period that he became
> friendly with Chang Ching-chiang, who was
> to become one of the most sinister char-
> acters in the Revolutionary Movement. He
> also came into contact with the leaders of
> the secret societies in Shanghai, which
> later on became very useful to him in his
> dealings with the Shanghai capitalists.[53]

T'ang, a prolific writer not always careful with
his facts and a political factionalist not always
friendly toward Chiang, met with no serious challenge to the essential veracity of this sharp-

24

tongued observation. In fact, his critical remarks were corroborated in the main by a sympathetic biography in 1929, when the political climate was still relatively permissive:

> Then came a period of rather riotous
> living, which few young men can escape.
> He was for the time working in the capa-
> city of an instructor in General Chen Chi-
> mei's army. But his work was light, tak-
> ing, on the average, two or three hours a
> day; and with a comfortable income which
> he was receiving there was much chance for
> moral degeneration. His friends, knowing
> his temper, and that persuasion would be
> futile, deplored this. . . . But the re-
> sults of his riotous living began to tell.
> Moreover, his hasty and violent temper ren-
> dered cooperation with others difficult. . . .
> Chiang is by nature obdurate. Not infre-
> quently he would fly into storms of tem-
> per before which few human beings could
> stand. Above all he was self-opinion-
> ated, highly so. No one could endure
> him, and by degrees he became more and
> more disagreeable to his associates.[54]

The central difference between these two accounts lies, of course, in their contrary percep-
tions and moral judgments concerning the very personality traits about which there is considerable
agreement in fact. While T'ang deplored Chiang's
presumably unredeemed moral degeneration, Cheng
and associates marveled at his character transformation. With the latter assessment missionary-
diplomat J. Leighton Stuart agreed, seeing before
him a repentent sinner: "For all I know the des-
criptions appearing in print of General Chiang's

25

manner of life and his summary treatment of political enemies up to ten years ago [1927] may all be true. If so, there is the greater credit to him because of the change since then for the better."[55]

In this chapter we shall examine Chiang's political involvement and personality development during the decade 1911-21, relying primarily on the "diary," despite its brevity and reticence on many events.

Chiang's revolutionary activities were sporadic throughout the period. When the clarion call was sounded in Wuhan on October 10, Chiang, accompanied by Chang Ch'ün, returned to Shanghai on the 30th, there to follow in the footsteps of Ch'en Ch'i-mei. Ch'en liberated Shanghai on November 3, whereupon he was elected by a revolutionary assembly as tutuh (governor) of the city, with Huang Fu as his chief-of-staff.[56] On the 5th Chiang led a dare-to-die contingent of about a hundred men from Shanghai to assist in the liberation of Hangchow, an uprising that quickly succeeded. Following this propitious start, Chiang immediately returned to Shanghai, where he formed, trained, and commanded the 5th Regiment (later the 93rd Regiment) as a part of the Kiangsu Army under Ch'en's command.[57]

Not long afterward Chiang took it upon himself to "liquidate" T'ao Ch'eng-chang, an influential leader of the Restoration Society (Kuang-fu-hui) in the Shanghai-Chekiang area and a potential threat to the authority of Ch'en Ch'i-mei. It has been said in justification of Chiang's act that T'ao, whose "revolutionary integrity had been held in contempt" by Chiang for several years, had acted against the interests of the party as early as 1908-09; it was also alleged that he was engaged in a plot to assassinate Ch'en.[58] In any event the critical moment is vividly depicted as having transpired in a hospital room in Shanghai: "The Chairman, angry beyond control, yanked out his pistol and killed [T'ao] with one shot."[59] Not wanting to embarrass Ch'en and probably shunned by party regulars as well, Chiang left for Japan in early 1912 to lead a brief private career as publisher and ardent essayist for the <u>Military Voice Magazine</u> (Chün-sheng tsa-chih). That winter he returned home and took a concubine named Yao.[60]

Several months elapsed before Chiang was called, in July 1913, to take part in the abortive Second Revolution against Yüan Shih-k'ai. Ch'en, who had been named commander-in-chief of the revolutionary forces in the Shanghai sector, ordered Chiang to gather the men who had served under him for an assault on the Kiangnan Arsenal. Chiang responded by seeking to infiltrate the 93rd Regiment he had once commanded, was arrested (or detained) near the Arsenal before he could establish contact with his former comrades, made his escape, launched an attack on the Arsenal with what forces he could put together, retreated into the International Settlement after sustaining heavy casualties, and surrendered his arms to the British authorities there. He then accompanied Chang Ching-chiang, the "sinister character" of T'ang Leang-li, on a trip to Nanking to see what cause they could support, found none, and returned to Shanghai the following day.[61] The entire episode lasted only about ten days, but for Chiang it probably marked the beginning of a close comradeship with Ch'en,[62] a hero prototype in those days, and with Chang, a king-maker by instinct.

27

For about a year after the collapse of the
Second Revolution, we know practically nothing
concerning Chiang except that he and Chang Ching-
chiang were admitted to membership in the reorgan-
ized Chinese Revolutionary Party (Chung-hua ke-
ming-tang) in Shanghai in October 1913,[63] and
that he subsequently joined many other revolutionaries in an exodus to Japan. Then, in May-
June 1914 he received his next assignment, to par-
ticipate in another uprising against Yüan in
Shanghai. The plot was discovered, and Chiang,
without much to do, was inclined "to pass away
the time at Chang Ching-chiang's place."[64] Soon
he received a summons from Ch'en ordering him to
proceed to Japan. That fall Ch'en sent him on a
mission to Manchuria to report on revolutionary
activities that never seem to have matured in that
far-away region, but Chiang did make use of the
time to volunteer a report to Sun on the two military issues of the European war and the anti-Yüan
movement.[65]

For a year after this brief and uneventful
mission to Manchuria, Chiang was again in Japan.
In February 1915 Hsü Ch'ung-chih, head of the party's Military Affairs Department, submitted to Sun
a recommendation for four field appointments in
China, including that of Chiang as Ningpo commanding officer of the Chekiang Revolutionary Army.
Sun approved the recommendations with the exception of Chiang, whom he believed, probably on the
advice of Ch'en Ch'i-mei, to be more useful to the
party's cause if kept in reserve for possible assistance to Ch'en in the Shanghai sector.[66] Thus,
Chiang remained in Tokyo, where during the months
of June to September he would pay occasional visits to the party's General Affairs Department and,
in the absence of Ch'en, confer with his deputy
Hsieh Ch'ih.[67]

In late October or early November, Ch'en,
then in Shanghai, finally called upon Chiang to
assist in yet another anti-Yüan uprising. He has-
tened to the field, urged upon Ch'en the assassination of the garrison commander of Shanghai, who
had twice thwarted Chiang's revolutionary schemes
in 1913 and 1914, and "hastily" drafted a plan
for the seizure of the government naval units
then stationed near the city. The assassination
plot was speedily and successfully executed, but
the ensuing land and "marine" assault ended in
quick and costly defeat.[68]

An interval of five months ensued, during
which time nothing specific is known about Chiang.
The "diary" then announces, rather grandilo-
quently, that he "led Yang Hu" in the spring of
1916 in the capture of the Kiangyin Fortress that
lay midway between Nanking and Shanghai, only to
find on the fifth day that he had been left alone
in the redoubt as a result of "mutiny from within." This event, for which there are varying
accounts,[69] has been compared by Chiang to the
Sian coup of 1936[70] and is revelatory of the sense
of persecution and alienation he often felt during his early adulthood. Not long after this reportedly humiliating defeat at the hands of his
own men, Chiang suffered on May 18 the loss of
his friend and mentor Ch'en Ch'i-mei by the hand
of an assassin.[71] While Chiang was never able to
transfer the warm personal relationship he had
had with Ch'en to any other living person, not
excepting Sun Yat-sen, his friendship with Ch'en
had led to an association with the revolutionary
movement and the organized party that was to develop into a unique opportunity, then into a cause
for service, and finally result in a complete
identity between the cause and the man himself.

29

In June Chiang was appointed by Sun as chief-of-staff to Chü Cheng, commander-in-chief of the so-called Northeastern Army in Shantung,[72] but by the time he arrived there the discordant army was already in the process of being dissolved consequent upon the death of Yüan.[73] Chiang soon proceeded to Peking "to observe the political situation" and by fall was back in Shanghai.[74] When Sun left for Canton in July 1917 to establish the military government, Chiang remained in Shanghai, where he shared lodgings with Ch'en Kuo-fu, a nephew of Ch'en Ch'i-mei. The "diary" also mentions in passing that he "maintained contact" with comrades from Chekiang, and it reproduces in full his plan for a two year northern expedition and a less ambitious plan for an invasion of Fukien and Chekiang. These plans he submitted to the new government in Canton on September 20 and October 1, respectively.[75] Beyond this we learn virtually nothing from the "diary" regarding Chiang's activities save that he was "often wary," that he "passed away his time with reading," and that he had "contact" with Chang Ching-chiang and a few other Chekiangese.[76] Elsewhere, we learn that Chiang might have been "concerned in armed robbery" in Shanghai on October 18[77] and that on November 1 he was named military counselor to Sun, now generalissimo of the military government.[78]

It was not until March 2, 1918 that Chiang left Shanghai for Kwangtung, reportedly in response to a call from Sun. There he received on March 15 a staff appointment as head of the Field Operations Department at the headquarters of the commander-in-chief of the Kwangtung Army under Ch'en Chiung-ming and on September 26 was "promoted" to a line assignment as commander of the Second Detachment of about one thousand men. Up to July 1919 he was rather regularly in the ser-

vice of the Kwangtung Army, though he did leave
his posts twice—in August 1918 for about a month
and again in March 1919 for about two months. But
during 1920 and 1921 he was in Shanghai and Chekiang more often than in the south, being present
in Fukien and Kwangtung for a total of only three
months in seven separate, brief appearances: 11
days from April 11 to 22, 1920; 24 days from July
12 to August 5, 1920; 31 days from October 5 to
November 5, 1920; 8 days from February 6 to 14,
1921; about 5 days in May 1921; about 2 weeks in
September 1921; and 9 days from December 22 to
the end of 1921 (when he remained until the following April).[79]

It is not always clear what Chiang's precise
role was when he was not in the south. Ch'eng
T'ien-fang, a student leader during the May Fourth
Movement, remembered Chiang as present but unin-
troduced at a meeting at Sun's residence in Shanghai in 1919. Chiang appeared interested in
Ch'eng's report on a projected strike by cadets
of the Yen-t'ai Naval Academy and, on hearing that
a cadet delegation had arrived in Shanghai in
search of support, interrupted Ch'eng to say, "You
might ask them to have a talk with me." At this
point he was introduced by Sun: "This is Mr.
Chiang Kai-shek."[80] We also know that in October-
November 1919 Chiang served as a courier-emissary
on Sun's behalf during a trip to Japan.[81] It has
further been said that in 1921 "he assumed the
duty of Mr. Sun's bodyguard, performing at the
same time a triple function as counselor, secretary, and in public relations."[82] But not much
more can be learned of his official activities
from 1918 to 1921.

As for Chiang's personal activities, we are
told that he did some reading and writing, made

31

frequent trips home, and associated with Tai Chi-t'ao during his stay in Shanghai in 1918; that he enjoyed chrysanthemums and exhibits among other things while in Japan in late 1919; and that he was often overtaken by illness during the first half of 1920 after he had returned to China: an eye ailment in January, typhoid in April, and dental treatment in June. In a letter to Hu Han-min and Wang Ching-wei, dated March 25, 1924, Chiang explained the etiology of his past, private excursions: "Everybody says that I am given to lust, but they do not know that this is a thing of last resort, in a state of utter depression."[83] From other sources we learn that in late 1920 he worked for a while "as a runner in a brokerage house."[84] At all events, by the time his mother died in 1921, Chiang was much improved physically.

We may further conclude from the "diary" that during the period 1911-21 Chiang was often impatient, uncompromising, impulsive, and ill-tempered, periodically manifesting symptoms of psychosomatic dysfunction and, as tutor Mao Ssu-ch'eng has diagnosed as early as 1902, giving evidence of being "wild and ungovernable . . . : one would think he had two different personalities." The record of his service in the army in 1917-19 shows that he was eager to make proposals,[85] that he was not satisfied with the quality and performance of the Second Detachment under his command, and that on one occasion he refused for three days to obey, though probably with good cause, a cease-fire order from his commander-in-chief, Ch'en Chiung-ming.[86]

Professional disagreements and temperamental differences with his colleagues began to have their

32

effect on Chiang by 1920, a year during which he seemed to undergo cycles of nervous strain. On April 16, "surrounded by small men, [he] suffered nervous pain"; on July 20 he manifested "uneasiness in manner" when Liao Chung-k'ai showed him a telegram from Sun; and on July 22 he "could not wait to hear" a telegram from Sun. On August 5 he left Fukien after receiving a wire from an unidentified source in Shanghai,[87] possibly also Sun. What these messages had to say is not made known to us, but it is known that on August 15 Chu Chih-hsin, that versatile and dedicated man respected by his comrades both for the fluency of his pen and for his courage in battle, wrote Chiang a letter adivsing him against alienating Ch'en Chiung-ming and Hsü Ch'ung-chih at this juncture and stating that he, Chu, would not assume a field command.[88] Chiang, however, was unmoved. On the 30th Sun, joined by Liao Chung-k'ai and Tai Chi-t'ao, personally urged Chiang to return to Kwangtung but failed in his effort because of Chiang's "obduracy."[89]

Three weeks later, on September 21, 1920, Chu died in the line of duty—or, more appropriately, beyond the call of duty—at Boca Tigris in the south. His death left the party devoid of a man of military capability but having no territorial power base of his own—with the single exception of Chiang. Thus, the very next day Sun in Shanghai turned again to Chiang, more diplomatically than before, and offered him the choice of going to Russia, Szechuan, or Kwangtung. Chiang declined to go to Russia on the grounds that he did not know well his prospective travelling companions. Nor would he volunteer to return to Kwangtung, which he had left on five separate occasions in two and a half years, for the reason

33

that "it would not do justice to myself even
though it may do good for the public cause." Instead, he was "willing" to go to Szechuan, which
had figured significantly in his 1917 proposal to
Sun for a northern expedition. But Liao, who was
also present, "forcefully persuaded" him to return south, where he was most needed, and on the
30th Chiang sailed for Kwangtung.[90]

He reached Swatow on October 5 and three
days later submitted a "comprehensive military
plan" to Commander-in-Chief Ch'en and Chief-of-
Staff Teng K'eng.[91] The extremely unpleasant atmosphere that must have prevailed during the ensuing days can be surmised from a letter Sun, obviously distressed by what he had learned of
Chiang's conduct, sent to him on the 29th:

> To my dear Elder Brother Chiang Kai-shek,
> When my elder brother Ch'en Chiung-ming
> fought back to Canton [against the Kwangsi
> clique of Ch'en Ch'un-hsüan earlier this
> month], he was devoting all his strength
> to serving our party and our country. We,
> on our part, are devoting all our strength
> to helping him. . . . All I ask of him is
> that he uphold my principles and my policy,
> that is to obey the democratic principles
> for which I have worked for these thirty
> years. Am I a tyrant who is pleased only
> when obeyed blindly? . . .
> The sudden and tragic death of Chu Chih-
> hsin is like the loss of my right or left
> hand. There are but few in our party to-
> day who have the dual qualities of military
> expertise and political dedication. Only
> you, my elder brother, are with us, you
> whose courage and sincerity are equal to
> those of Chu Chih-hsin and whose knowledge

34

of war is even better than his. But you
have a fiery temper, and your hatred of
mediocrity is too excessive. Thus it often
leads to quarrels and renders cooperation
difficult. As you are shouldering the
great and heavy responsibility of our
party, you should sacrifice your ideals a
little and try to compromise. This is
merely for the sake of our party and has
nothing to do with your personal principles. Would you, my elder brother, agree
with this? Or would you not?[92]

Biographer Hsiung notes: "This letter from Sun
Yat-sen was not entirely without effect. It
stopped Chiang Kai-shek from leaving Chen Chiung-
ming for seven days."[93] Upon his departure for
Shanghai on November 6, Chiang nonetheless felt
impelled to leave behind a denunciatory letter
for Ch'en:

You, my Commander-in-Chief, are an expert in strategy and are also full of
experience; if you had not been ill-
advised you would never have done this;
if you had trusted me, you would never
have done this. And if those who were
marching forward with their men at the
front had a little common sense, they
would have followed the dictate of reason
and corrected the wrong decision; this is
the way to help and cooperate. But, instead, their minds were so full of jealousy and prejudice that they had no regard
for the coordination of the whole plan,
nor any concern for the success or failure
of the entire campaign. I am straight-
forward and dare not act contrary to my

conscience in disclosing my views to you.

I came at your call this time really because of the death of Chu Chih-hsin. That
made me fight side by side with you against
one common enemy. Also because of un-
settled conditions in Kwangtung, I decided
to disregard myself and follow the leadership of others as my duty to the party.
For the sake of loyalty and public spirit,
I came forward without the least selfish
thought.[94]

On November 12 Chiang disembarked at Shanghai and "immediately called on Sun to report on
conditions in Kwangtung." He left for Chekiang
the next day, and Sun, in anticipation of a return to Kwangtung to lead the military government once again, telegraphed him on the 15th and
16th, "urging his speedy return to Shanghai."[95]
Chiang responded on the 17th, explaining that he
could not comply with the request because "my
mother is very ill and I am too" and inquiring
whether "I could be apprised of the broad outline
of the party's position."[96] Sun departed for
Canton on the 25th, apparently without replying
to Chiang's inquiry.

On December 7 Chiang appeared in Shanghai,
where he had "frank and open talks with comrades
for several consecutive days." These talks must
have been inconclusive, for a week later Chiang
returned to Chekiang. The "diary" then informs
us that on the 25th Tai Chi-t'ao, his old friend
from Chekiang, went to see him in Feng-hua and
urged him to go to Kwangtung, and that on the 27th
Chiang "accompanied Chi-t'ao to Shanghai, return-
ing home the next day."[97] What transpired in the
course of their journey to Shanghai was an explosive altercation between the two intimate

36

friends, an argument that, as the letters between them in the following month vividly reveal, left Tai terribly distraught and Chiang "wild and ungovernable."

The exchange of letters between Chiang and Tai in January 1921 constitutes indispensable and unmistakable evidence of Chiang's character and psychological condition during his early thirties. It was a state of mind of which he had become conscious in 1919, but over which he had seemed unable to exert any meaningful control. Because these letters are invaluable historical documents as well as evidence for our investigation of Chiang's personality, a careful review of them is well justified.

On January 5, a week after Chiang's violent display of emotion, he wrote what apparently was meant to be an apologetic note to Tai. Protesting his friend's "unbearable" sternness, he engaged in some self-analysis of his "bad temper," complained of being persecuted and abandoned, and summed up the situation by invoking the wisdom of Tseng Kuo-fan as a curative for both:

> The other day when the trouble started, you, my Elder Brother, seemed to me to be very stern in both your voice and color: I could not get a word in edgewise, and so I felt it unbearable. You, my Elder Brother, have always had a great affection for me, that I know. Generally, whenever you have persuaded me to do, or dissuaded me from doing something, I have never failed to follow your advice.
> But although I have been extremely patient with you, my Elder Brother, I have a bad temper and am usually lacking in good

manners. As I have lately been taken so
much advantage of and have suffered so much
at the hands of others, I became uncon-
sciously rude the other day, bursting out
all at once. At a time when we are enduring the same hardships and vowing that we
shall face good or bad fortune unflinch-
ingly together, I feel, after careful reflection, most ashamed of myself. I know
myself that I have been ridiculous. When
a man has been so lacking in self-control
and so rude, how can he have the face to
see his beneficent teacher and helpful
friend again? So I enclose a copy of
Marquis Tseng's letter to his younger
brother Yüan-fu, reproaching him for having quarreled with P'eng Hsüeh-ch'in, which
I think could be used with great profit as
a mirror for both of us. If our friendship is going to be further improved after
this, then it is a blessing in disguise.
I hope you will forgive my misbehavior and
never be niggardly in giving me your instruction, which I shall consider myself
most fortunate to receive.[98]

Tai's lengthy reply, dated January 14, was
both poignant and penetrating. He protested his
own innocence, accused Chiang of being "incorrigible" and irrational, and deplored his friend's
tendency to put self before service. Reminding
Chiang that authoritarianism was a thing of
the past, Tai advised him not to mind the conduct
of the nation if he could not mend his own personal conduct and pointed in contrast to the magnanimity of Sun Yat-sen. He called to Chiang's
attention the fact that the Kuomintang was "progressing steadily" and doing far better than his

38

angry friend might have thought, implying that
the party was certain to succeed with or without
him. For Chiang to offer his service to the
party at this time, Tai suggested, would be both
correct and personally advantageous:

I have read your kind letter. I do not
know myself how it happened that I offended
you that day, my Elder Brother. For you,
my Elder Brother, I have nothing except a
heart full of sincerity. Even my persuad-
ing you to go to Canton was prompted half
by duty and half by my concern for your
personal advantage. When I met with your
seemingly unreasonable fury, I felt most
dejected. I blamed myself for having com-
plicated matters, and my heart was still
aching when I sailed home in my boat. . . .
Your sphere of work, my Elder Brother,
is active service of a responsible nature.
To shut your gates and live inside your
house is to care for nobody but yourself.
The other day you said, "To urge me to go
out and work is to urge me to shorten my
life." When I heard this remark, I was
much pained, all the more so because I
myself was actually worried at the thought.
The old proverb says, "Rivers and mountains can easily change, but human nature
is difficult to alter." You, my Elder
Brother, are extremely self-willed to an
almost incorrigible extent. Whenever you
are despondent and in a state of intoxication, you let your anger go unchecked.
In dealing with people in that way, you
court calamity; or at the least you will
find it most damaging to your career.
The present is quite different from

ancient times. Where is there to be
found a minister of remonstrance who
observes everything you do from day to
day? Even if there were such a man, how
could he be certain that you would follow
his advice? . . . If you, my Elder Brother, cannot bear things with fortitude
and hold firm, setting your mind on the
way of the golden mean, uprightness, and
peaceableness and reflecting on these
things three times a day, how can I, who
am not without affection for you, dare to
persuade you to go out and work? During
recent years I have repeatedly urged you
to go to Kwangtung, and in doing so I
believed I loved you much. But the other
day, after I heard what you said and later
reflected on it once and again, I dared
not urge you any longer. That was also
because I loved you much. Your letter
indicates that I was angry with you. I
have nothing but love for you. That
love may take the form of heartache but
never anger. As for my advice to you,
patience and fortitude, the way of the
golden mean, uprightness, and peaceable-
ness--these are the proper ways of conduct even if you remain at home. Toward
members of your family and your servants,
your townsmen and friends, you must all
the more control your temper, never using
a harsh word when things happen contrary
to your wish. . . .

You, my Elder Brother, must reflect that
the work of Mr. Sun is progressing steadily
toward success. From the day he started
the revolution, the propagation of his
principles in China has probably progressed

40

faster than that of the revolutionary
doctrines of any other nations. Now,
what are Mr. Sun's assets? Both Chang
Ching-chiang and I think that faithfulness, kindness, and peaceableness are the
qualities in which he excels. We have
never seen him do to others what he would
not like done to himself, nor bear enmity
toward someone who has offended him personally. And his dislike of putting
people to death cannot be equaled by anyone in political circles in this or any
other country. The way of the golden
mean, uprightness, and peaceableness are
in his nature. As for his great wisdom,
knowledge, and thought, they are the means
through which he cultivates the excellence
of his character; they are not part of his
character. . . . I do hope that you, my
Elder Brother, and I will endeavor to follow his example.[99]

Chiang's rejoinder, which was written on the
20th, noted that Sun's greatness lay more in his
"straightforwardness" than in "faithfulness, kindness, and peaceableness." Sharp-tongued and obviously externalizing his own feelings, Chiang
complained of "your marked prejudice and sentimentality and the sharpness of your words," sug-
gesting further that Tai was not nearly as kind
and peaceable as he thought himself to be. He
also reminded Tai of the ill-feeling that existed
between him and Ch'en Ch'i-mei and raised the
searching, somewhat caustic question: "Are you
not strict with others while being generous with
yourself?" He went on to say that the real-
politik unfolding in Kwangtung was beyond the com-
prehension of Tai, who was too "sincere" or too

naive to understand the "complications of the situation" and "their treatment of me." Chiang defended his refusal to return to the service of the military government as being not a question of "narrow-mindedness" or "conceit" but a simple case of standing up for one's own dignity, rights, or perhaps relative advantage in a given situation. He explained that his much misunderstood expression "to live alone in the mountains or wilderness" should be construed figuratively, not literally. He had no desire, he said, to avoid responsibility and "to live in selfish comfort" but asked only that he be allowed to undertake tasks leading to "a clear-cut and fundamental solution," which in the specific instance meant that "my going to Kwangtung is entirely dependent upon a definite date being set for the mobilization of the Cantonese Army against Kwangsi province." For the moment, he would commit himself only in principle to a trip south.

In order to gain a more sensitive understanding of the impulsive and assertive nature of Chiang's character as well as a clearer picture of his self-perception, his letter of January 20 is given in part below:

> I think the best quality in Mr. Sun's personal relationship is his straightforwardness; thus people respect his dignity and are grateful for his kindness. That of Chang Ching-chiang is that he never utters a sarcastic word; thus people who have offended him feel ashamed of themselves.
> You, my Elder Brother, are expecting too much from your friends; also you are too sharp in your reproach and not generous enough; that is where you cannot quite reach the height of Mr. Sun or of Chang

Ching-chiang. Yet, despite the fact that I treat you as my revered friend and beneficent teacher, my feeling of respect and fear toward you has never reached that which I feel toward Mr. Sun and Chang Ching-chiang. This is because we are of about the same age, because we have been very familiar for so long, and because I am quite used to your reproaches. Also it is largely due to your marked prejudice and sentimentality and the sharpness of your words.

In Kwangtung province there is a peculiar atmosphere, and a man like Mr. Sun, who treats people with sincerity, is not to be found. The complications of the situation there, my Elder Brother, you could not totally comprehend. As for their treatment of me, they throw me over when they do not need me and beckon me to come back when they do. What kind of thing is that? How can I bear such treatment? Am I too petty and narrow-minded? Perhaps. But while we should not be conceited, neither should we demean ourselves. Should we attach ourselves to bandwagons so as to frequent the doors of those in power? And should we be so greedy for position as to ask for pity from those heartless acquaintances? Would that be the proper thing for us to do who want all our comrades to uphold their dignity?

You, my Elder Brother, once told me that Ch'en Ch'i-mei was jealous of you, and therefore the two of you did not get on well. You would not even want to translate Japanese for him. If someone had forced you to work with Ch'en Ch'i-mei, I know you would have protested and thought it

outrageous. Today your forcing me to work
with Ch'en Chiung-ming is exactly the same.
Are you not strict with others while being
generous with yourself? Should we change
places, you would hardly know what to
think. Therefore, I ask you, my Elder
Brother, to forgive me a little.

In your letter you say that I consider
your urging me to go out and work as forcing me to shorten my life. This is a
mistake or a misunderstanding on your part.
I said only that I had a bad temper, un-
suitable for society; that I must leave
my friends to live alone in the mountains
or wilderness, and then perhaps I might
live longer. I said this because I remembered your constant advice and blamed myself for offending people at every turn on
account of my temper; it would seem best
for me to retreat to the mountains and the
caves in order to avoid further mistakes.
I was blaming myself for my bad temper, not
you for urging me. I feared only the con-
sequences of my going; I did not say that
I would never go. In short, I do not wish
to live in selfish comfort and ease, nor to
separate myself from the world. Though it
is true that I fear people's jealous tongues
and want to avoid their enmity, it is not
true that I prefer to live as a coward
rather than to die courageously. Tasks
which lead to a clear-cut and fundamental
solution I will undertake with pleasure;
work which lacks reality and produces no
result I decline to do.

The trouble with me in society is that I
go to extremes. Therefore, I have lifelong,
sworn, intimate friends but no ordinary

44

boon companions or social acquaintances. The same applies to my words and actions. In this connection I am reminded of the proverb, "Rivers and mountains can easily change, but human nature is difficult to alter." . . . [Yet it must also be said that] man's strengths and weaknesses are largely formed by his environment; it is not utterly impossible that his nature should change somewhat.

My going to Kwangtung is entirely dependent upon a definite date being set for the mobilization of the Cantonese Army against Kwangsi province. I wonder whether you, my Elder Brother, and I will be traveling together? The fact that I have decided to take this trip to Canton certainly demonstrates that I respect others' opinions and disregard my own.[100]

By the time this letter to Tai was written on January 20, Chiang's decision to join Sun in Kwangtung had been made for at least ten days, though he had sought to keep it something of a secret in order to improve his own bargaining leverage in what appeared to be a largely untenable position. On January 10 he had dispatched three communications. One was a seven hundred word position paper on a northern expedition, submitted apparently on his own initiative "to Sun and other comrades." In it he stressed, as he had done before, the overarching strategic value of Szechuan and proposed, either optimistically or recklessly, a corollary maritime expedition from Kwangtung to Chinwangtao in Hopei province. Nothing, however, was mentioned, directly or by implication, about his return south or his own role in the expedition.[101] Given the weakness of his position, his greatest strength unquestionably lay in his ability to keep Sun in doubt.

Chiang's second communication was a letter to his influential friend and benefactor in Shanghai, Chang Ching-chiang, who must have been apprised of the serious altercation between Chiang and Tai. Chiang began by admitting to a lack of "cultivation, respectfulness, and constancy." Pleading guilty to being "stubborn," "rude," and "offensive," he commented that Tai "Chi-t'ao loves me, but he is unaware of my shortcomings; besides, he is given to sentimentality in his conduct and is overly stern in his rebuke of others." Chiang concluded with an explanation of his impending departure for Kwangtung and four attendant conditions for undertaking this trip:

> My going to Kwangtung this time is really forced by Mr. Sun's orders. I am unreasonably made to follow them although it is well known that Kwangtung is not a suitable place for me to stay long, that the work is utterly impossible for our party to carry out. This is indeed a most unfortunate situation, which preys on my mind incessantly, and so I dare to reveal it frankly to you.
>
> Mr. Sun sent me a telegram on the 7th ordering me to go without delay. My views are: one, the day of mobilization will be the day that I embark; two, Tai Chi-t'ao must accompany me; three, please quickly remit the funds relative to Chou Jih-hsüan and Shao Yüan-ch'ung; and four, I will serve in a private capacity and will not accept any official commission. Please telegraph [Mr. Sun] a reply on my behalf and put it in a roundabout manner so as not to offend his feelings.[102]

46

Through Chang, Chiang wanted to convey to Sun, albeit in a "roundabout" way, a rigid posture.

The third communication was a "confidential" reply to Ku Ying-fen, a close associate of Sun for many years.[103] In this letter Chiang questioned Ch'en Chiung-ming's sincerity in desiring his (Chiang's) return and raised grave doubts concerning Sun's prospects for building a viable government in Kwangtung. Nevertheless, he promised to set sail within two weeks and said he would accept either staff or line assignment in the army at Sun's discretion, although he hinted at his own preference for an opportunity "to train a crack unit within half a year for battle in central China." The four conditions he had asked Chang Ching-chiang to communicate to Sun were not mentioned; apparently, they were not meant to be sine qua non for his departure but rather indicated his habit, in the words of one analyst, of "pushing his interests as far as possible and exacting every ounce of advantage in any situation."[104] The letter concluded:

> As for the time of my departure, I will leave no later than the 24th via the S.S. Chung-kuo. Please do not divulge this information to outsiders. At this time it is yet best to say that I will not come to Kwangtung. Has Mr. Hu Han-min returned to Kwangtung? Please let me know in your next letter. Kindly show this letter to Liao Chung-k'ai, Wang Ching-wei, and Hu Han-min.[105]

In promising to go south without setting conditions, Chiang wanted to present through Ku a flexible, if also zigzag, posture to Sun. His request that Ku disclose the contents of his letter to the three "insiders," was an attempt to soften

the hard feelings he had created by an earlier
letter of January 4 to Hu and Liao, in which he
had said quite rudely that he would go to Kwangtung "on the day Mr. Sun commences [the expedi-
tion] by issuing the order for mobilization, provided I have not left the country [by that
time]."[106] Chiang had apparently concluded that
persistent defiance might end the dialogue altogether, whereas a soft, somewhat ambiguous stand
could open the channels of communication.

The desired result came on the 12th, when
Sun sent him a telegram which, while showing signs
of annoyance, was by no means harsh in tone or
content. Sun reminded Chiang of "your promise to
come to Kwangtung" and urged him "not to delay
any longer" in joining the "impending" campaign.
At this point, Chiang reverted to a rigid posture
and replied stiffly: "You, sir, have been in
Kwangtung for fifty days, but not a single order
has been issued for mobilization. That is what I
am awaiting. As soon as the date for the start of
the campaign is decided, I will come to serve you
without waiting for your call."[107] Three days
later, on the 15th, Chiang heard from Ch'en
Chiung-ming, who explained in some detail that
"preparations for the campaign against Kwangsi
will soon be completed" and asked that he accept
a commission to lead the central column.[108] On
the 21st—only one day after he had written Tai
Chi-t'ao that his departure was contingent upon
the issuance of mobilization orders—Chiang responded temperately to Ch'en. After giving a "comprehensive view of the overall military situation," he promised to leave "within ten days to
serve you in a private capacity."[109] Apparently,
Chiang had now concluded that this was the far-
thest "extreme" to which he could push his case.

48

On February 6, 1921 Chiang arrived in Canton.
He soon found that "there was no consensus" on
the pending campaign against Kwangsi and left
Canton on the 14th, "greatly embarrassed."[110]
From Chekiang Chiang wrote to Sun on March 5 to
voice his now well-known denunciation of Ch'en
Chiung-ming: "As for the present situation in
Canton, you, sir, can only hope that Ch'en Chiung-
ming will remain within the general scope and not
exceed the limits [of his authority]. If you expect him to take your orders at the critical moment and to defend the party against its foes,
[you will find] he is not the man."[111] On March
29 Sun again urged Chiang to return and partici-
pate in the planning for the "western expedition"
against Kwangsi. Chiang replied: "As the date
for mobilization has not been decided upon, of
what use is it for me to come? In fact my presence would only add to the difficulties confronting you. I have decided to postpone my trip."
There is no record that Chiang responded to Sun's
telegram of April 8, but when Sun wired on the 21st
to inform him that mobilization orders had been
issued the preceding day, Chiang immediately replied that he would start his journey within ten
days. Chiang left Chekiang on May 10, arriving in
Canton ten days later.[112] But on the night of the
24th "he dreamed of a landscape of snow, white and
boundless. He awoke from the dream trembling,
sensing that it portended ill for his mother. He
felt ill at ease and hurried home." On June 14 his
mother died.[113] Whether Chiang would have stayed
longer in Canton without the dream is impossible
to tell with certainty, but it is on record that
his next trip to Kwangtung lasted for only two
weeks, a period marked by frequent fits of passion.

A telegram from Sun came on June 23, and his
plea for Chiang's early return was reinforced by

49

wires from Yang Shu-k'an, Wang Ching-wei, Hu Han-min, Chang Ching-chiang, and Shao Yüan-ch'ung. Chiang, in mourning and with thoughts of building a shrine for his deceased mother, does not seem to have replied. A month later, on July 20, Sun again sent word asking for his speedy return, the urgency of the request being impressed upon him by telegrams from Hsü Ch'ung-chih, Yang Shu-k'an, and Hu Han-min. On August 10 Chiang started his journey "with reluctance," stopping over at Shanghai for more than ten days. There, "one stormy day, he was seized with thoughts for the safety of his mother's bier, apprehensive of its being flooded. That night he dreamed much, and the following day he sped home, . . . to find with much relief that the coffin was undamaged in a five-foot flood." After nearly a month he renewed his journey on September 3, having sent Ch'en Chiung-ming on August 15 an "extensive discussion" of matters relating to Wu P'ei-fu, who was then in control of Peking. On September 13 he arrived in Canton, called on Sun, and visited Commander Hsü Ch'ung-chih to decide on the date for the commencement of the expedition. On September 17 "he reached Nanning [in Kwangsi], went to see Commander-in-Chief Ch'en, listened to what he had to say, became extremely irritated, and left in a rage to catch the next boat leaving Nanning." After seeing Sun and other party leaders in Canton, he left for Hong Kong and eight days later departed for Shanghai.[114] When Sun himself arrived in Kweilin, Kwangsi on November 15 and established a headquarters from which to launch the so-called First Northern Expedition, Chiang responded to Sun's call, this time to stay for a much longer period of four months.[115]

This detailed and rather extensive inquiry into Chiang's politics and personality in

the years 1911-21 enables us to say that he was
an impulsive man unable to exercise rational control over his behavior in moments of stress. It
would also appear that the psychological disequilibrium so characteristic of him in his early
thirties was due in some measure to the loss of
his benefactor and hero model, Ch'en Ch'i-mei, in
1916, the year Chiang attained the age of 30 sui.
The one significant life model he had found since
he left for Japan in 1906, he now lost. There
was no ideal living substitute for Ch'en in sight.
Chang Ching-chiang, the person who came closest
to replacing Ch'en as Chiang's mentor, was hardly
a model for him. Chang had Ch'en's self-assurance
but was devoid of the military flair that so at-
tracted Chiang to Ch'en. Tai Chi-t'ao "loved"
Chiang most, as Chiang said, but he was too young
to serve as a model; in any event, in Chiang's
eyes he was too "sentimental" and far too un-
realistic in this "cruel world" of uncertainty
and change. Hsü Ch'ung-chih, Chiang's immediate
superior in the Kwangtung Army and a close friend,
was "too disorganized and particularistic and one
on whom I personally would not place much hope."[116]
Yang Shu-k'an, an associate of Ch'en and then of
Chang, was "too lazy" and "not worth the bother."[117] As for Sun Yat-sen, his merit lay in his
"straightforwardness," a personality trait Chiang
himself possessed; but Sun was too undiscriminat-
ing, in Chiang's view, in dealing with such persons as Ch'en Chiung-ming, who was "not the man"
for the party at a critical moment.

The evidence presented heretofore thus
suggests that the impatient and intemperate Chiang,
as he reached the age of thirty, was a self-willed
and persecution-haunted young man whose emotional
instability was the product of a deep sense of
alienation experienced since childhood and of an

inability, after the death of Ch'en Ch'i-mei, to be identified with a living hero who could provide him with existential satisfaction and psychological security. This being the case, he sought to identify himself with the living dead, such as Tseng Kuo-fan, who could rise above the bounds of time in splendid perfection.

From the "diary" for the decade following 1911 we may observe, further, a calculating, venturesome man who, through reading, reflection, and meditation, was finally able to establish his identity. By late 1921 he began to find the quintessence of life's purpose summed up in the traditional teachings of China's ancient past, a purpose mirrored in the life of his new-found model Tseng Kuo-fan and one which he was certain would reach new heights in his own life. It took all these years, with such furor of life and with all the calming effects of intuitive contemplation, for him to find himself, and for others to learn of what stuff he was made.

Chiang's formal education in classical literature had ended, to all intents and purposes, in 1905, when he became acquainted with the works of Tseng Kuo-fan and Sun Tzu's Art of War. From 1906 to 1911 he spent most of his time in Japan preparing himself for a politico-military career in China. We have little knowledge of what reading he did on his own during these years, being told only of Tsou Jung's The Revolutionary Army, which he "devoured day and night" in 1908. In 1912, following his assassination of T'ao Ch'eng-chang, he was again in Japan. Before his return to China at the end of the year, he made two efforts to advance his intellectual (and political) interests:

he studied the German language in order to prepare himself for further education in that country; and he published the Military Voice Magazine,
for which he wrote the foreword to the first issue.[118] This foreword and five other articles he
wrote for the magazine constitute the earliest
extant essays by Chiang and provide us with our
first glimpse into his instrumental beliefs, as
opposed to his philosophic beliefs, in matters
political and military.

In the foreword he dismissed the then
popular notion of a universal commonwealth (shih-
chieh kung-ho ta-kuo) as mere "idealistic talk"
and characterized the world as then constituted
as one of "armed peace." Power and national interest, he wrote, were the motivating forces that
shaped the China policies of the imperialist nations, which included Britain, the United States,
Russia, France, Germany, and Japan. Furthermore,
in relations between unequal states such as China
and the imperialist powers, the guiding principle
for China could only be the Bismarckian policy of
blood and iron. Now that China's "internal" problems had in his view been solved by the overthrow
of the Manchu dynasty, the revolutionary efforts
of the nation should be directed toward solving
its "external problems," among which the military
issue was "the most important."[119]

He developed his thoughts concerning the
overarching military question in an article on
military administration. In the interest of centralization, he argued strongly against the institution of provincial armies and stood firmly
for the separation of civil and military authority
on the provincial level. In the interest of national integration, he suggested regional military
districts as the most efficacious organizational

53

means of meeting the dual requirement of functional unity and structural diversity. He dismissed as irrelevant the criticism of over-centralization on the national level and pointed in reply to the historical experience of China "over the past three thousand years," during which there had been no national unity without military centralization, and to the precarious international situation confronting China that allowed it no other alternative. To avoid both Bonapartism and anarchism, he openly espoused "enlightened despotism" of a type that would combine "Washington's ideals" with "Napoleon's methods" and "democratic thought" with "revolutionary spirit."[120]

The other four articles had to do with border defense and China's foreign policy, with a stress on the dangers posed by Japanese and, especially, Russian imperialism. In the July issue he commented that China's northern defenses were more crucial than its southern defenses for the reason that British interests in Tibet were commercial rather than military. He warned that Russian imperialist designs in Mongolia and Manchuria had not ceased with the Russo-Japanese War and that Russia and Japan had subsequently reached an understanding to coordinate their aggressive designs in China. In a military encounter with Japan, he noted, China would have to rely on land forces and especially on a protracted war strategy in order to deplete Japan's manpower and financial resources, while in a war with Russia, China should prevent the penetration of its northern frontiers by the enemy and at the same time launch an attack in Central Asia. And in preparation for a war against combined Russian and Japanese forces, which he felt was entirely possible, China would be well advised to adopt a policy of "armed peace,"

allocating from one-third to one-half of its
national budget to the military establishment.
Were military expenditures directed "entirely" to
the strengthening of its land forces without benefit to the navy, a respectable army might be developed of 600,000 well-trained and well-supplied
troops capable of coping effectively with any fore-
seeable military engagements. As to the existing
units under the personal command of various military leaders, Chiang demanded that they be dis-
banded as a demonstration of patriotism in this
national endeavor.[121]

Three months later Chiang wrote an article on
the question of Mongolia and Tibet, deploring the
inability of the government to act decisively to
suppress border revolts and expressing the opinion
that the recovery of China's rights in these ter-
ritories necessitated the expulsion of British and
Russian influence. He noted realistically the
geographical and logistic difficulties that a
Tibetan expedition would encounter and daringly
proposed that China "stake all on a single throw"
and go to war with Russia at a time when it was
deeply involved in Balkan affairs.[122] Soon thereafter Chiang wrote another tract, in which he singled out Russia as the principal aggressor in
China and recommended that China exploit the conflict of interest between Britain and Russia and
seize the opportunity of Russia's Balkan predica-
ment to take a greater initiative in recovering
China's rights.[123] Then in December he wrote what
appears to have been his last article for the magazine. While continuing to direct his attention
toward the recovery of Mongolia and preparation
for war against Russia, he stressed the wisdom of
laying a diplomatic foundation for this war and
the necessity of taking "ten or several scores of
years" for its preparation.[124]

55

The six articles demonstrate that Chiang, ambitious and anxious at the age of 25, was highly motivated to keep abreast of world events and that his knowledge of world affairs was probably based on the extensive reading he had done in prior years. Furthermore, we are impressed, as we scan the horizon of his life, by the degree to which his political ideas, beliefs, and priorities persisted in later years: the idea of benevolent dictatorship, the stress on national unity and political centralization, the primacy of the military, and the precedence of nationalism ("external problems") over democracy ("internal problems") and of political revolution over social revolution. Additionally, his distrust of foreign nations, no doubt objectively justifiable, was consonant with and indeed sustained by his misanthropic predisposition. Finally, the narrowness of the range of his views and the persistence with which he maintained them are characteristic of the obsessional-compulsive personality type that he was.

From 1913 to 1915 Chiang was in Japan on three separate occasions. During these stays abroad he "formed a resolution for learning, sitting daily in contemplation, reading, and practicing calligraphy." His readings were of two types: military texts, which provided him with "a foundation in military science," and the works of Wang Yang-ming, Tseng Kuo-fan, and Hu Lin-i, which formed "the basis of my political science" and the source of his philosophic beliefs. Indeed, he was so enthralled with the teachings of Marquis Tseng that he is said to have finished in 1913 the 174 chüan of Tseng's complete works (Tseng Wen-cheng kung ch'üan-chi), a feat that resulted in an eye ailment. His contemplation centered on the word "remorse" and all that it implied, and he was es-

pecially attentive to the old adage, "Do not
look at what is improper; do not listen to what
is improper; attain a composed mind and a composed
spirit."[125] The sensitive Chiang, so intent to
prove himself and make himself count, must have
been painfully aware of the tempting voices of
evil and of the necessity to summon up the best in
himself in order to combat the deadliest of sins,
"insincerity."

Chiang was relatively active in party work in
1916 and it may be assumed that this was not a
year for reading. Nor is any reading list given
for the year 1917, when he associated intimately in
Shanghai with comrades from Chekiang. But it was
recorded that during these years he would nonetheless engage in meditation "in his quiet hours," his
thoughts turning to, among other things, the Men-
cian notion of expansive spirit and Marquis
Tseng's exhortation on serenity. He would also
offer silent prayers for: "(1) the reconstruction
of the party and the nation, (2) the amelioration
of the people's livelihood, (3) the moral rectitude of the people, (4) health and longevity for
his mother, (5) the safety of Ch'en Ch'i-mei and,
after his death, the repose of his soul, (6) success and achievement for his two sons, (7) daily
advancement in wisdom and virtue, and (8) success
in his personal career."[126] Sun Yat-sen did not
yet have a special place in his private thoughts.

The year 1918 was noteworthy for the simul-
taneous enlargement of Chiang's public responsibilities and private studies. Perhaps his in-
creased interest in learning was the by-product of
the challenge of a new career in closer proximity
to Sun. His readings continued to lengthen and
broaden during the otherwise unstable and tempes-
tuous years of 1919-20. He read avidly, according

57

to his own account. In addition to the inevitable
books on military science and military affairs, he
became interested in publications identifiable
with the new thought movement and the new education. His readings in the new literature included
books on science (astronomy), modern history and
social science (a general history of the West, a
biography of Napoleon, an outline study of political science, a history of the Russian revolution,
three books on economics, geography, several at-
lases, a study of the World War), European literature and philosophy (Ibsen, Tolstoy, and Dewey),
Western languages (Russian and English), and three
liberal journals (Hsin-ch'ao or Renaissance, Hsin
ch'ing-nien or La Jeunesse, and Tung-fang tsa-chih
or Eastern Miscellany). But traditional Chinese
literature must have been most congenial to him
and probably received his primary attention. For
relaxation, he read Shui-hu chuan (All Men Are
Brothers), Ju-lin wai-shih (An Unofficial History
of the Literati), and the more popular poems of
the T'ang and Sung dynasties. His reading in history was far more extensive, including the histor-
ies of the Sung, Yüan, and Ming dynasties (identified as Sung chien, Yüan chien, and Ming chien),
two works relating to foreign affairs (Fan-hai chi-
lüeh and Ting-i ts'ung-k'an), the exploits of Tso
Tsung-t'ang in Chekiang (P'ing Che chi-lüeh), a
history of the Taiping Rebellion (T'ai-p'ing t'ien-
kuo wai-lüeh), a general history of China (Li-tai
t'ung-chien chi-lan), and the Spring and Autumn
Annals (Ch'un Ch'iu). The philosophical and related wroks read during this period he mainly
scanned by way of review: the Four Books; the Classics; the writings of the philosophers of the Chou
and Ch'in dynasties, especially Chuang-tzu; the
complete works of Hu Lin-i (Hu Wen-chung kung i-
chi), with particular attention to his letters;
Tseng Kuo-fan's letters to his family (Tseng Wen-

cheng kung chia-shu); the complete works of the neo-Confucian idealist Lu Chiu-yüan (Lu Hsiang-shan ch'üan-chi); a book of maxims and proverbs (Ts'ung-hsün chai-yü; and miscellanea.[127]

Fortunately for our understanding of the relevance of these works to his psychological and ideological frame of mind in those years, Chiang also recorded his reflections in the "diary." In 1918 his meditations, influenced as they were by the notions and concepts he had acquired from Mencius, the Great Learning, and the Idealist school of Neo-Confucianism, showed a marked proclivity toward transcendance in interpersonal relationships, self-reliance in the pursuit of a life purpose, and introversion in character cultivation. During the "evening hours of tranquility" his thoughts would revolve around the following precepts of Wang Yang-ming: (1) Render dignified and majestic all the manifestations of one's nature, and thus be unaffected by worldly turmoil; (2) dispel worldly desires and preserve moral rectitude; (3) elevate the mind and thought through the extension of knowledge and the investigation of things; (4) cultivate meditation and right concentration; and (5) avoid confusion and anxiety.[128] By 1919 he was of the belief that his self-rectification should go beyond the negative concept of "remorse" and instead stress the values of serenity (ching), attentiveness (ching), tranquility (tan), and constancy (i). To this end he besought Sun to inscribe the four words, to which he added his own commentaries, as a constant reminder to himself.[129] His reflections during these two years suggest that he had acquired a deeper intellectual appreciation of traditional virtues, though he still lacked the refinement of mind that must be had in order to put virtue into the real life that was to be lived. They also

suggest that his appreciation of the virtues of
serenity, attentiveness, tranquility, and constancy tended to heighten in proportion as he experienced increasingly frequent periods of mental depression, and then emotional outbursts, in the
course of coming into contact with problems far
more complex than those he had faced under the
aegis of Ch'en Ch'i-mei.

There is no record of Chiang's self-examination in 1920, but on February 9 and September 4
of that year he wrote his first recorded letters
to his ten-year-old son Ching-kuo. The advice
Chiang gave in these didactic letters was at once
reminiscent of his own conduct and attitude when
he was himself a boy of ten and indicative of his
current meditative attainment. In the first letter he wrote: "At home, obey the instructions
of your grandmother and mother. In talking
and walking your manner must be serious; never
conduct yourself with levity. In the classroom,
you must listen quietly and attentively to what is
taught and try to comprehend the lessons with utmost care." A second letter advised: "At home
you must be filial to your mother and grandmother
and respectful to your elders. When you walk,
don't be frivolous and make sure to be serious.
Don't be querulous when you play with your school-
mates."[130] Obedience to authority and avoidance
of evil—the one a positive commitment to order
and the other a concomitant withdrawal from chaos
—appear to have been two cardinal virtues to
Chiang.

The year 1921 was a year of vacillation and
then decision. It was a year of many quarrels and
hurt feelings, for it was also a time when party

leaders and personal friends made repeated requests, indeed demands, for his services. As he stood at a crossroads in his life, faced with a choice between commitment and withdrawal, he turned to "meditation and right concentration" to overcome the oppressive forces of "confusion and anxiety." His self-assessment and object appraisal resulted in a political commitment to Sun and the Kuomintang, notwithstanding disagreement over policies and differences in personality. Thus, after his mother's death in June, he made arrangements in November for "separation" from his wife Mao and concubine Yao, as well as for the division of the family estate between his sons Ching-kuo and Wei-kuo. While supporting evidence is sparse, it is within the realm of possibility that, given Chiang's belief in cosmic unity and in the prophetic nature of dreams, he might well have construed his mother's demise as a sign that heaven had released him from familial obligations in order to commit his life to the Kuomintang and the nation. Be that as it may, he was by year's end a free man, unburdened by familial responsibilities and avowedly ready "to dedicate my energy to the revolution with all my heart." On December 22 he arrived in Canton and the next day was summoned by Sun to proceed to Kweilin to assist the party leader himself in the First Northern Expedition.[131]

The year 1921 was also a year of psychological reorientation. The despair and sense of persecution he had felt in the past had given rise to recurrent, unreasoning displays of passions; but they had also produced an emotional crisis from which he was to emerge a self-assured man with unbounded faith in himself and in the mission he was prepared to undertake, given the proper conditions. Although he was frequently to relapse into doubt

and anger, we begin to see by late 1921 signs
pointing toward greater stability in his behavior,
toward an integration of his personality and his
social environment. In any event, before he was
forty there was "no doubt" in his mind that he
was China's man of destiny.

This personality analysis of Chiang in 1921
is confirmed by his own words in the "diary" for
that year. In the spirit of the Great Learning
he wrote that "the only way to avoid confusion
of the heart [i.e., anxiety over the unknown] is
to conduct affairs according to [regulated] procedure and to engage in reading in [regulated] se-
quence." He also said, with a Chuang Tzu-like
twist: "To look at no-form, to listen to no-
sound, and to seek happiness in the spatial void;
[thus cultivated,] there is no question but that
my nature will be purified." Finally, he declared
in a transport of enthusiasm: "With an expansive
and illumined mind, a firm and courageous spirit,
I will cultivate a glorious stature so as to become illustrious throughout the world. It is evident what will ensue therefrom."[132]

Thus, by late 1921 the essential Chiang had
begun to emerge. What he did thereafter may be
regarded as the fulfillment of a fixed purpose in
accordance with a regulated procedure. He continued to learn from both traditional and modern
literature, from both Chinese and Western sources,
in reading and in private expository sessions, but
what he learned thereafter was learned in the
light of his fixed purpose and was used to rein-
force, at best to refine, his fixed concepts.[133]
With all things fixed in their proper places, his
mind gained a measure of composure and became more
responsive to his will and less subject to the aberrations of his passions. By the sheer power of

62

his will, he was to transcend the masses, made "formless" in his sight, so that he could be their moral teacher. He was to rely on his own judgment and instinct rather than the counsels of his friends and advisers,[134] made "soundless" to his ears, so that he could be their supreme arbiter. He began to withdraw from the pleasures of the world, to lead a regulated personal life, and to introvert his affects into the "spatial void" within himself, so that he could maintain that requisite psychological balance in the performance of his moral and political duties.

Chiang's idealized self-image, together with his feelings of guilt and persecution, is mirrored in several entries in the "diary" for 1923, one of which tells of a remorseful soul: "My parents' expectation of me is that I should become a complete man, but my lowly self this day is replete with transgressions and evils. How can one not be pained by this? I will renew myself daily from now onward in order that I may nurture the divine elements in my nature." Another entry reveals a tormented Chiang impelled to make a choice between the avoidance of life and the fulfillment of heaven's will: "During the first half of this year I suffered a prolonged eye ailment to the point where I could neither read nor fulfill my normal functions. I was so vexed that several times I thought of taking my own life. But then I would comfort myself by saying, 'It is the will of Heaven that I should undertake the mission of the party. How is it possible that it would destroy my eyesight? All I need is to recuperate until health is restored.'" Once during the second half of 1923 he again sensed persecution and abandonment, whereupon he effected an almost total withdrawal into himself: "Counting with the fingers

of my hands, who, besides Mr. Sun, treats me with
sincerity? Those I once thought could be trusted
turn out to be all the more untrustworthy today.
In all things one has only oneself to rely on."
He also said: "Of all the people in the world,
Mr. Sun is the only one worthy of being a dear
friend. Aside from him, I have only my children
to love. The rest are all bores." The last reference is the most revealing both in terms of his
own character-building in the twenties and of the
character of his ideological affirmation in the
thirties:

> One morning I awoke to examine my past
> transgressions. [I became aware that] the
> reason I was despised was my excessive, friv-
> olous jests, and [that] the reason I aroused
> jealousy in people was the haughtiness that
> remained unexpurgated in me. The cause of
> this [psycho-]pathology was light-minded-
> ness and a quick temper. Henceforth I must
> needs practice meticulous self-control and
> amiability in my personal conduct. I would
> rather be ridiculed as archaic and doltish
> than be regarded as wild and ungovern-
> able.[135]

Thus, it may be said that Chiang's long journey in quest of identity, which he began in 1906
at the age of 20, was finally completed by 1921-23
when he was in his mid-thirties. By then, he had
found himself by discovering the limitations and
possibilities of his own personality. He had also
learned what national politics implied and required
and how his personality could respond to the com-
plexities of Chinese politics and the requirements
of his time. His prescription for himself was
"meticulous self-control" and his prescription for

himself in relation to the nation was "to undertake the mission of the party" and "to be illustrious throughout the world." If this meant a
narrowing of perspective for him and the introduction of an authoritarian style of leadership
for China, this was what must be. For as he
said, "I would rather be ridiculed as archaic and
doltish than be regarded as wild and ungovernable." His personality structure, he realized,
allowed of practically no other political style.
Having so perceived himself in this political
role, he presented himself on the political stage.
His friends and the party leaders, in full knowledge of his assets and liabilities, accepted him.
In fact, they demanded his services in the name
of revolution, both because of and in spite of
him.

V. POLITICAL RECRUITMENT: SUN YAT-SEN
AND CHIANG KAI-SHEK

When Chiang Kai-shek decided in late 1921 to
commit himself to a career in the Kuomintang, he
did so only after being persuaded that he could
find a place within the immediate orbit of Sun's
activities and that he would be in a position to
effect "clear-cut and fundamental solutions." Before Sun's death in March 1925, however, Chiang
was to experience many more disappointments, to
find himself in several excruciatingly disagree-
able confrontations with the party leadership, to
offer his resignation or simply leave his post on
several occasions, and to be haunted by many more
bad dreams. Yet despite disagreements with Sun
and quarrels with others, his career moved forward
in almost unbroken ascendancy, due chiefly to his
"straightforwardness," decisiveness, earnestness,
and his military qualifications and leadership
ability, as well as to the relatively universalistic orientation that resulted largely from his
lack of a personal politico-military base, and,
somewhat belatedly, to his demonstrated loyalty to
the party leader.

Sun began to take a more active interest in
Chiang following the death of Ch'en Ch'i-mei in
May 1916. Ever in need of qualified military personnel, Sun assigned him in June to assist Chü
Cheng in what proved to be an evanescent anti-Yüan
campaign in Shantung. And "kindly" man that he
was, Sun, upon learning in September of the birthday of Chiang's mother, sent her a tablet inscribed
by Chu Chih-hsin, commending her for her "expertise in child rearing" (chiao-tzu yu-fang).[136]
Upon her death in 1921, Sun was represented at her
funeral by Chiang's close friend, Ch'en Kuo-fu,
and had carved on her tombstone the inscription

"Tomb of Mother Chiang."[137] During the troubled years that intervened between 1916 and 1921, Sun had hoped that Chiang would serve where the party's need was the greatest, in Kwangtung and Fukien. But this turned out, as we have seen, to be highly unsatisfactory for Chiang and most annoying for his associates. The death of Chu Chih-hsin in 1920, however, made Sun's search for military talents ever more urgent even as it made Chiang's prospects of service brighter than before.

For some time Sun had been aware of the restive young officer's desire to travel abroad and to train a "crack unit." He may not have known of Chiang's studying Russian in 1919-20,[138] but he knew of Chiang's interest in making a trip to the revolutionary Soviet fatherland. Thus, on September 22, 1920, during one of Chiang's frequent leaves from the Kuomintang military service, Sun offered him the choice of going to Kwangtung, or Szechuan, or Russia, although in all likelihood Sun really wanted him to serve in the army in Kwangtung. Chiang did not choose to go to Russia at this time, for reasons mentioned earlier, but his interest persisted. For instance, it is known that on January 15, 1921, Sun's associate Ku Ying-fen wrote to urge Chiang to return to Kwangtung instead of going to Russia, and this information must have been passed on to Sun.[139] Then on March 5 Chiang wrote directly to Sun to express, among other things, his view of the soundness of the Soviet policy of internal unity before external resistance and his admiration for the Russian spirit of self-reliance in international relations.[140] Sun doubtless was also aware of Chiang's desire to head a military training program instead of taking up staff or line duty, for Chiang had intimated this in his letter of January 4 to Hu Han-min and Liao Chung-k'ai and had brought it up directly in his letter of January 10 to Ku.[141] What was not known to Sun was the degree of Chiang's commitment to the Kuomintang, a commitment Sun was to discover in the course of 1922.

As mentioned before, Sun ordered Chiang on November 9, 1921 to leave Chekiang for the south, and again directed him on December 23 to proceed from Canton to the Generalissimo's Headquarters in Kweilin.[142] Before Chiang reached Kweilin, however, he had learned something of Sun's plan for a northern expedition that caused him to "regret the trip as being premature." When he did see Sun on January 30, 1922, they discussed the date for launching the expedition and the removal of the headquarters to Shaokuan in northern Kwangtung. Then suddenly, in late March, General Teng K'eng, the one person on Ch'en Chiung-ming's immediate staff whose loyalty to Sun was not in doubt, was murdered. His assassination was generally believed to have been instigated by Ch'en and thus seemed to portend ill for Sun. On March 26 Sun called an emergency meeting at which it was decided to suspend the First Northern Expedition in Kwangsi and return the expeditionary forces to Kwangtung.[143] This decision was, of course, in general accord with Chiang's view.

Significant differences still existed between Sun and Chiang, however. At the emergency meeting Chiang had recommended not only the return of the army to Kwangtung, but also an immediate campaign to suppress Ch'en before the northern expedition was resumed.[144] On April 5 Chiang took leave of Sun and went back to Kwangtung, intent upon implementing his own recommendations. On the 14th he felt "uncomfortable throughout the night" because of Ch'en's "change of mind," and on the 15th he was "still not able to sleep [and became]

68

very sick."[145] Five days later he learned, as
he had feared, that Sun had accepted Ch'en's resignation as commander-in-chief of the Kwangtung
Army and governor of Kwangtung but had insisted
on his continued service as minister of war. This
turn of events could only mean that Sun had finally rejected Chiang's advice in preference for an
uneasy alliance with Ch'en and had decided to continue, as before, to place priority on the northern expedition, despite Ch'en's known unreliability. His proposal having been rejected, Chiang
decided to leave for Shanghai on the 23rd and only
reluctantly agreed to stay on when Sun reportedly
said to him: "If you leave at this time, Hsü
Ch'ung-chih and I will not be able to function at
all. What use is the body if it is without a
soul." Immediately following this conversation,
however, Chiang was faced with such "unceasing
provocation and jealousy from certain quarters"
that he changed his mind again and "resolutely
decided to leave," whereupon he boarded a steamer
for Shanghai the same day. That evening "he
talked incessantly in his sleep and, in a loud
voice, led his troops across a river in his
dreams; . . . all the passengers in the boat were
aroused." He arrived in Shanghai on the 27th and
returned home the following day "to visit Mother's
grave."[146]

On May 6 Sun established his headquarters at
Shaokuan to resume the northern expedition. As
Chiang had anticipated, the army's rear was left
exposed and Canton fell under the control of
troops allied with Ch'en Chiung-ming. During the
ensuing month Chiang sent several communications
to Kwangtung, pressing the argument he had pre-
viously presented at the emergency meeting in
Kwangsi. On the 9th he wrote to Liao Chung-k'ai,
"forcefully arguing" the importance of Sun's re-

turn to Canton. On the 25th he sent telegrams to
Wang Ching-wei, Hu Han-min, Liao Chung-k'ai, and
Hsü Ch'ung-chih to express his "anger over the
occupation of Canton by the Ch'en clique" and to
reiterate the necessity "to consolidate the rear
before making plans for the northern expedition."
And on June 1 he argued in a well-reasoned letter
to Hsü that the unification of China was predicat-
ed upon the party's control of Kwangsi and especially of Kwangtung and that the consolidation of
Kwangtung would require the return of Kuomintang
troops from Shaokuan "to resolve the fundamental
problem that was Canton." Regardless of what
Ch'en might do or say, he concluded, the party
must act without "hesitation or equivocation,"
for "he who makes the first start rules others."[147] By then Sun must have realized the grav-
ity of the situation or the cogency of Chiang's
argument, for that very day he returned "to pre-
side over his command from the presidential palace
in Canton." But he must also have acted with
great "hesitation" and "equivocation," for he returned only with his bodyguards, thus compounding
the danger by having himself exposed to the whims
of mutinous troops. Sun indeed had cause to cable
Chiang on the 2nd, urging him to hasten to Kwangtung "to help me in this moment of imminent peril
[ch'ien-chün i-fa--30,000 catties hanging by a
single hair]." On the 16th Ch'en struck.[148]

Sun managed to escape to the warships at
Whampoa, from where he personally directed a hope-
less campaign to recapture Canton. On the 18th,
in desperate need of whatever military aid he
could find, he wired Chiang, "Matters critical;
hope for your speedy arrival." But aware of
Chiang's well-known aversion to the political environment in Kwangtung and of the impossible position in which he found himself, not to mention his

disregard for the recommendations made by the
sensitive officer in the past, Sun probably had
little hope that Chiang would respond.[149] When
Chiang in fact boarded the command ship Yung-feng
on the 29th, they "looked at each other in great
surprise. Ch'en Chiung-ming, who apparently had
succeeded in causing friction between Chiang and
Sun, was equally surprised at Chiang's return.
Wang Ching-wei wrote to Chiang on July 1:
"[When] Ch'en heard that you had returned, his
face turned blue and he said: 'With him [Chiang]
by the side of Mr. Sun, there will certainly be a
great many devilish ideas.'"[150]

Why Chiang came to Sun's aid, without delay
or attempt to bargain, can only be speculated upon. Perhaps his adventuresome nature drew him to
where the action was; perhaps an aroused sense of
chivalry made him want to be of some personal service to Sun in distress. It is possible, too,
that Chiang was simply manifesting his vengeful
instincts against the deeply resented Ch'en,[151] or
that he saw this as a unique opportunity to im-
press upon Sun that he had been right all the
while in his distrust of Ch'en. And given what we
have learned of Chiang's life up to this point, it
may also have been that he had emerged from his
identity crisis resolved to "cultivate a glorious
stature" and to illumine it through Sun's Kuomintang, the party his friend Tai Chi-t'ao had impressed upon him as being the most promising political organization in China. Whatever the reason
or reasons might have been, immediately upon receiving Sun's telegram, Chiang is said to have
written to Chang Ching-chiang in Shanghai, entrust-
ing to Chang his family and various other matters
in the event of his death. Chiang then traveled
to Kwangtung via Shanghai.[152]

71

For one and half months Chiang was in close
attendance on Sun.[153] As none of the party leaders remained on board the Yung-feng,[154] it appears
likely that the two men had a unique opportunity
to establish a close relationship and their association seems to have been unmarred by bickering
or interpersonal tensions. When Sun decided on
August 9 to leave Kwangtung waters to await a
more propitious moment to return to Canton, Chiang
accompanied him to Shanghai aboard the Russian
vessel S.S. Queen.[155]

In retrospect, it is clear that Chiang's decision to come to Sun's aid during the Canton coup
of mid-1922 was an important factor in his subsequent career in the Kuomintang. In October of
that year he published a personal account of the
events from June 15 to August 15, for which Sun
wrote a preface.[156] This book, together with a
picture of Chiang and Sun allegedly on board the
Yung-feng,[157] established Chiang as something of
an "old faithful" and made all the more convincing
his later claim to legitimacy as Sun's successor.
For instance, on the centennial of Sun's birth in
1965, Chiang proudly recounted the experience and
declared: "Because of my day-long attentiveness,
there arose between us a kind of wordless rap-
port." According to Chiang, Sun told him one
night: "I know I have only ten more years to live
at the most. But you will have at least 50 more.
. . . If nothing untoward happens in the future,
it is not too much to expect you to carry on the
struggle for 50 more years for the sake of our
principles."[158] Chiang's presence, furthermore,
seems to have made a strong impression on Sun and
probably dispelled some of his doubts concerning
Chiang's role within the party. In spite of the
fact that Chiang remained uncompromising in his
relationships with other party members and that

his military service in the south continued to be
erratic during the year following the Canton coup,
Sun in due time found ways to create opportunities
suitable to Chiang and useful to the party. Mean-
while, on August 12, two days before they reached
Shanghai, an event occurred that was to be of
great significance for both Sun's program and
Chiang's career. Adolph Joffe arrived in Peking
in a favorable political climate to promote relations between Moscow and the Peking government and
to develop contacts with nongovernmental circles
in China. [159] We may assume that Sun and Chiang
learned of Joffe's warm reception either on board
ship or shortly after they disembarked at Shanghai. Subsequent contacts between Sun and Joffe
were eventually to result in a reorganization of
the Kuomintang and the formation of a party army.

Nine days after arriving in Shanghai, Chiang
left for Ningpo.[160] On August 27 he wrote to
Chang Chi, who at this time had wide contact with
leftist and Communist elements in China. Chiang
spoke of having met a certain "Mr. Chu" just before leaving Shanghai and of having discussed a
"certain matter" with him and inquired whether Mr.
Chu could "proceed first." Chiang also wanted to
know if "the other party is in fact able to help
me" and the "degree" to which it was willing to
support "our requests and aspirations," and suggested that he, Chiang, might "go north" to ex-
plore the matter further.[161] We do not know the
identities of "Mr. Chu" or "the other party," but
they presumably were not unrelated to Joffe's
mission in China. Three days later Sun himself
wrote to bring Chiang up to date on developments
in the south. He apprised him of a recent conversation with the representative of a certain person, presumably Joffe, on "certain matters" relating to "major problems in the Far East and the

73

methods for their resolution" and expressed hope
for Chiang's early return to Shanghai.[162]

In the meantime, on August 29 Chiang also
wrote a long letter to Liao Chung-k'ai and Wang
Ching-wei, in which he gave a detailed explica-
tion of his views on the military situation confronting the Kuomintang and proffered some advice
on party affairs. Concerning military matters,
he commented on the timing of an expedition
against Kwangtung, which he said should begin
within three months, and in any event not later
than November. To accomplish this primary objective of reestablishing a revolutionary base in
the south, the party, he declared, should make
maximal "utilization for our own ends" of the
armies of other warlords. To this end, he urged
that, because of the relative strategic importance
to Kwangtung of Fukien, Hunan, Kiangsi, and Kwangsi, the party ally with the warlords of these provinces to form an inner circle of military
strength in preparation for a final assault
against Ch'en Chiung-ming; and he further pressed
for an entente with the Chekiang faction of Lu
Yung-hsiang (allied with the Anfu Clique of Tuan
Ch'i-jui), the Fengtien Clique of Chang Tso-lin,
and the Chihli Clique of Ts'ao K'un in order to
forge an outer circle of politico-military
strength to influence the course of events in the
south. It is an interesting commentary on his political style of later years that in this overall
strategy Chiang singled out only two persons as
enemies of the party—Ch'en Chiung-ming as the internal enemy and Wu P'ei-fu as the external enemy
—and once he had clearly identified his enemies
he was to an exceptional degree able and willing
to establish working relationships with otherwise
incompatible political elements. Concerning party
affairs, Chiang was of the opinion that the party

74

could not be "rehabilitated" without first revising its constitution. In the process he felt that the induction of "purposive youths" would enhance the influence of the Kuomintang and that the party's Political Council must be constituted to maintain a centrist posture between old and new party members.[163]

Chiang's exposition on the recapture of Kwangtung demonstrates the kind of expertise in military affairs and familiarity with broad national issues that had commended him to Sun. His comments on party matters, coupled with the fact that they were directed to the progressive Liao and Wang rather than to the conservative Hu Hanmin, suggest that he was aware of Sun's current thinking on party reorganization and that he was already making an initial adjustment in his own public posture. But Chiang remained in Ningpo, as if he found it difficult to voice his opinions in the give-and-take sessions of the party's inner councils, or perhaps because he believed his arguments to be so conclusive that little need existed for further consultation.

Responses from Shanghai were soon forthcoming. Liao and Wang replied that while they agreed with Chiang's views in principle, events had been developing so rapidly that his presence in Shanghai for ready consultation was necessary. Wang also asked him to take charge of military affairs and assured him that he need not be involved in social events but would be consulted on political matters.[164] On September 9 Chiang put in a momentary appearance in Shanghai. He "stayed over for two nights and hurriedly returned" to Ningpo.[165]

During this brief stay Chiang is known to have visited Chang Ching-chiang at the latter's residence,[166] but he did not see Sun, Liao, Hu,

and possibly not Wang. On September 12 Sun wrote
to apologize for having been overwhelmed by other
matters and an interminable stream of callers,
explaining further that Liao, Hu, and Wang were
soon to depart for Japan, Shenyang, and Tientsin,
respectively. Sun said that by the time he was
able to receive Chiang, he heard that Chiang had
already left. He expressed the hope that Chiang
would return to visit him for a few days.[167]
Chiang, however, had left Shanghai "in a very bad
state of mind," saying to himself that "this is
not the place to stay for [even] one day," for
Shanghai, far more than Peking, was nothing but
"a huge oven for the manufacture of evil men."[168]
Thus, Chiang ignored Sun's polite, but casual,
letter, and remained in Ningpo to write his account of the Canton coup.[169] Not until early October, when he learned of definite movements in
the south, did he leave Ningpo. On the 4th he
appeared in Shanghai long enough to make his in-
tentions known, then left promptly for sightsee-
ing in Wuhsi and Soochow. As he must have anticipated, a telegram arrived from Sun on the same
day, summoning him to return immediately. After
three days Chiang finally presented himself before Sun,[170] who appointed him on the 18th chief-
of-staff to the Eastern Route Rebel Suppression
Army under the command of Hsü Ch'ung-chih in Fukien.[171]

Chiang lost no time in making his way to the
field of action in Fukien, where he arrived on the
22nd.[172] On November 11 he resolved with characteristic certitude: "This time I will shoulder
myself, single-handed if needs be, the responsibility for fighting the rebels and slaughtering
the traitors to avenge the treacherous deed they
have done to us. Should this inspire jealousy or
create misunderstanding, I am willing to accept

it, no matter how difficult it may be nor how many friends I shall offend. I will not stop until the aim is achieved."[173] On the 19th, however, Sun received word that Chiang was about to leave his post. He immediately wired Chiang, "You must accomplish your mission, however difficult the task may be,"[174] and followed it up with a letter on the 21st:

> I have just seen your letter to Hu Han-min and Wang Ching-wei in which you said "if there is no progress at all within ten days then there is nothing for it · · · ," etc. Pooh! What rubbish you talk! Since I could not go to Fukien myself, I have entrusted you with the responsibility of punishing the traitors. How could you so quickly think of giving it up like that?
>
> Things do not happen as we wish eight or nine times out of ten. Success always depends upon your fortitude and persistence, your disregard of jealousy and hard work. If you give up when there has been no progress within ten days, then you will never succeed in doing anything.[175]

Although the letter reached Chiang on the 24th, it did not deter him from leaving for Shanghai the same day. Twenty-four days elapsed before he was persuaded to go back to Fukien, but once more he returned to Shanghai, only three weeks later on January 7, 1923.[176]

Chiang remained in Shanghai for twenty-one days, from the 7th to the 27th.[177] Again it appears that he failed to see Sun and other key party leaders, then preoccupied with matters relating to party reorganization. On December 16, 1922 and January 1-2 following, while Chiang was in Fukien,

Sun had taken steps to introduce a new party platform, a revised constitution, and a party manifesto, all for the purpose of broadening the
social and ideological base of the Kuomintang.
In the ensuing days, when Chiang was in Shanghai,
Sun, aided by Liao Chung-k'ai, was busily engaged
in seeking a consensus with leaders of provincial
party organizations and must have found it nearly
impossible to see Chiang. On the 21st, following
a busy round of caucuses, Sun was finally able to
announce the appointment of new men, including
the Communist Lin Tsu-han, to major posts in the
various departments of the party's Central Executive Committee.[178] The next day Sun met with
Joffe, and four days later they issued the joint
manifesto that marked the Kuomintang's new pro-
Soviet orientation and presaged a more basic
structural reorganization of the party.[179]

Perhaps because Sun had always considered
Chiang a military man, he had therefore excluded
him from these significant developments within the
party. Being present in Shanghai in the midst of
these occurrences, however, must have sensitized
Chiang to the new directions in which the party
was headed and the new career opportunities they
opened up for him. Thus, on the 26th Chiang wrote
a long letter to Liao--both were then in Shanghai
--which, besides offering the inevitable commentaries on the military situation in south China,
expressed his first concrete views on party-
government relations as they might be applied to
the transitional period in China's political development.

The letter, though not well-written, was well-
conceived. It was concerned with three aspects of
Kuomintang political leadership--political posture,
political priorities, and functional differentia-

tion within the governing body--and thus is
revealing of Chiang's political style in the not
too distant future when he came to play the primary role on the Chinese political stage. Pro-
ceeding from the central proposition of maximal
"utilization for our own ends" of the existing
military and political variables in China, he
mildly reproached Sun for his "overly rigid
views," which, Chiang said, had rendered it difficult to "manipulate" otherwise malleable elements
in Chinese politics. Rather than insisting on its
own narrowly-defined positions and expecting
others to fall in line, the Kuomintang should, he
suggested, make it possible to effect working relationships with all factions, or nearly all, provided they did not contradict or detract from the
immediate objective of the party. As long as this
central objective--presumably Kuomintang primacy
in the power matrix--was kept inviolate, all other
issues could be relegated to positions of secondary importance and compromise should be possible.
The question of progressivism versus conservatism
thus faded into relative insignificance in relation to the primary consideration of political
power, particularly when Chiang raised the question directly: Which should come first for the
party--principle or power?

     In answering this crucial question, Chiang
pointed to three courses of action theoretically
open to the Kuomintang. First, the party could
delude itself into believing that in the immediate
future it would be possible to obtain simultan-
eously ideological purity and organizational supremacy. Such a feat, while not impossible, would
take ten to twenty years, he commented, and "was
not attainable in China today." Second, the party could give priority to ideology and the inter-
nalization of prescribed value-attitudes among an

expanding membership. Should this be the course chosen, the party would have simply to work steadily and patiently toward the defined goal until it was finally realized, at which time political power would be within easy reach of the party. But in that case, the party must refrain temporarily from engaging in a power struggle, as it had all too obviously failed to do. The third alternative, which Chiang recommended as the "easiest" and "quickest" means of reaching their objective, was for the Kuomintang to emphasize political power over party principle. This did not mean a total disregard of ideological vigilance; it would, however, require, as he had said at the outset, a greater measure of political and tactical compromise as the price to be paid for the speedy attainment of political power.

In order to protect ideology from being subverted in the process, Chiang raised his third major point: functional differentiation between the party and the government. For at least five years, he said, party cadres should function within the party as the overseers of government administration. The party of believers, in other words, was to serve as the policy-making and policy-reviewing body, while a government of practitioners would fulfill policy-executing, administrative-managerial functions under the supervision of the party. With such an arrangement, the party could afford to bring within the operational fold of the government "Chinese-style political talents" such as T'ang Shao-i, Li Lieh-chün, Sun Hung-i, and T'an Yen-k'ai. The experience and influence of such men would broaden the base and increase the effectiveness of the government; at the same time, the functional differentiation of governing power between policy formulation and routinized management would ensure the ideological incorruptibility of the party and the faithful pursuit of defined objectives, especially, he suggested, if men like "Liao and Wang Ching-wei would place themselves between the government and the party." He added:

In recent years I have come increasingly to feel that party members and politicians are not only different in kind but also in the skills in which they excel. To insist upon political management by party members would not only limit the scope [of politics but would immediately cause] outsiders to avoid [politics]. Furthermore, it would result in certain ill-feelings in the party's relations with the public and in opposition from the [larger] community, making difficult [at the same time] the realization of desired results. This, I believe, is the one insight I have.

Of necessity the letter dealt with each issue on an abstract or suppositional level, for Chiang had not been in touch with Sun, Liao, and other active party leaders during his three-week stay in Shanghai. Thus, the letter began by inquiring, "What are the recent developments in Kwangtung?" and ended with, "Who will remain in Shanghai after Mr. Sun's departure [for Canton]? How many will go with him? Will you be accompanying him? . . . If you approve of this letter, please let Mr. Sun read it."[180] The following day, Chiang returned to Ningpo.[181]

On January 29 Wang Ching-wei responded to Chiang's letter, which Liao had shown him. But while Wang expressed complete agreement with Chiang's views, the tone of his letter suggests

what must have been the consensus of the party
leadership--that the place for Chiang in the party was in the military.[182] Thus, when the Military Council was formed on February 3, Chiang was
made one of its thirteen members.[183] On the 7th
Chiang "went to Shanghai in response to Wang
Ching-wei's request, stayed over for two nights,
and promptly returned" to Ningpo. What transpired between Wang and Chiang during these two
days is not explained in the "diary," but it
appears likely that Chiang was disturbed not so
much over his uncertain role in the party in the
future as over his place in the military at the
moment. Chiang had committed himself to the party in late 1921 in the belief that he would find
himself close to Sun and the center of power. But
his position as of early 1923, aside from his
membership on the new and untried Military Council, was that of chief-of-staff to Hsü Ch'ung-chih
in Fukien. In fact, with Sun about to return to
Kwangtung in the wake of victory of a sort over
Ch'en Chiung-ming, Chiang was unwilling to serve
under Hsü, just as he had chosen not to serve under Ch'en a year before. Therefore he wrote Sun
on the 12th, expressing great anxiety at the
thought of Sun's "going alone" to Kwangtung and
requesting Sun to inform Hsü of Chiang's own in-
dispensability there. The point was repeated in
telegrams to Hu Han-min, Wang Ching-wei, and Yang
Shu-k'an on the 13th.[184]

In the meantime, events had been developing
rapidly in Kwangtung. Sun's representatives in
Hong Kong, Tsou Lu and Teng Tse-ju, had been successful in rallying under the Kuomintang banners
the Kwangsi armies of Shen Hung-ying and Liu Chen-
huan, the Yunnan armies of Yang Hsi-min and Fan
Shih-sheng, and smaller units of Kwangtung troops
commanded by Ch'en Chi-t'ang, Teng Yen-ta, Lü

82

Ch'un-jung, and others. Under pressure, Ch'en
Chiung-ming effected an orderly withdrawal of his
troops from Canton on January 15-16 and returned
to his stronghold at Hui-chou (Waichow). Sun
made plans to leave for Canton on the 27th, the
day after Chiang wrote his long letter to Liao,
but dissension among the victorious provincial
troops and the questionable loyalty of the powerful General Shen Hung-ying caused him to postpone
the trip at the last moment. When a semblance of
order was finally restored in February, the con-
fident Sun once again made ready for a triumphant
return to Canton. On the 13th he sent a telegram
to Chiang, apprising him of the impending trip
and adding somewhat casually, "If you cannot come
in time [to leave with me], please board another
ship and come quickly." Sun left Shanghai on the
15th and landed in Hong Kong on the 17th.[185]

Upon his arrival in Hong Kong, Sun discovered
that the situation in Kwangtung was far from en-
couraging. The mutineer Ch'en had been forced
out of Canton, but his army remained intact in
eastern Kwangtung, where he continued to be a potential threat to both Canton and Fukien. Furthermore, suspicion that the Kwangsi General Shen
Hung-ying was in collusion with Sun's enemy Ch'en
Ch'un-hsüan and the Peking government remained un-
dispelled. Shocked into renewed realization of
the fundamental unreliability of warlord armies as
instruments of the Kuomintang, Sun must have re-
gretted the indifferent tone of his invitation to
Chiang. At all events, on the 18th, the day after
his arrival in Hong Kong, Sun appointed Chiang
chief-of-staff to the Generalissimo's Headquarters
and telegraphed to say: "Hu Han-min and Tai Chi-
t'ao both have important assignments at the present time. . . . The need for your assistance
here is urgent. Anxiously request your immediate

arrival. Do not delay. Your appointment as
chief-of-staff has been announced."[186]

But despite the desirability of this appointment, which would have placed Chiang in the personal service of Sun, he still refused to go, and
repeated urgings from Sun, Liao, Ku Ying-fen,
Yang Shu-k'an, and even Chang Ching-chiang were
of no avail.[187] On March 15 Hu Han-min, Wang
Ching-wei, Tsou Lu, Lin Yeh-ming, Lin Chih-mien,
and Hu I-sheng went to Ningpo to implore him to
go to Kwangtung. Chiang took them on a sightsee-
ing trip for several days, "accompanied them to
Shanghai" on the 19th, and then returned to Ningpo on the 27th.[188] Having gained the assurance
that he was wanted in Canton, he now wished to
know what he was wanted for. By instinct inclined to maximize his returns in any given situation, he wanted to be assured that the campaign
against Ch'en Chiung-ming would be carried to its
logical conclusion, that his voice would be heard
in deciding personnel matters within the party and
the government, and that he would not be relegated
to a position from which he would be unable to
effect "clear-cut and fundamental solutions."

On March 5 he wrote to remind Sun that a decision on priorities must be made: "If it is not
possible to cope with Shen Hung-ying's army, it
would be better to be lenient toward [it] and commit our total efforts to first exterminating the
traitor Ch'en."[189] On the same day he also wrote
Yang Shu-k'an and Ku Ying-fen to stress the same
point, adding that Ch'en must be exterminated even
if it required the mobilization of all available
forces and the temporary "abandonment" of Canton
to small garrison units. He felt constrained to
respond to Sun's call in this moment of desperate
urgency, he explained, notwithstanding the eye

84

ailment said to have been troubling him for the past two months.[190] On the 21st, while in Shanghai with Hu Han-min, Wang Ching-wei, and others, he sent Sun a telegram, said to be "missing," to press the need for financial reforms.[191] From the "diary" it would appear that Chiang received no response during the next two weeks. If that was indeed the case, he must have wondered whether he had pushed his case too far. On April 6 Chiang appeared in Shanghai and made moves to break the silence. He telegraphed Hsü Ch'ung-chih on the 7th to say that he would "make a trip to Kwangtung in my personal capacity." The next day he wrote Yang Shu-k'an that he had made definite plans to leave for Canton. He also urged that Hsü's army return to Kwangtung to lead in a coordinated attack against Ch'en Chiung-ming and that Liao Chung-k'ai be put in charge of financial affairs, and asked whether both orders could not be issued "before I start my journey."[192] Sun responded immediately and acceded to some of Chiang's wishes: Chiang was permitted to resign his posts as chief-of-staff to Hsü on the 9th and as chief-of-staff to the Generalissimo's Headquarters on the 10th.[193]

Chiang left Shanghai on the 15th and arrived in Canton on the 20th, where two military situations must have received his attention: the suppression of Ch'en Chiung-ming and the revolt of Shen Hung-ying. Chiang lost no time in involving himself in the campaign against Ch'en and, though holding no official post save his sinecure on the Military Council, made plans and issued orders. These were challenging days, during which he was responsible to no one but Sun, but they were also trying times that tested anew his ability to work directly under Sun. In late May Ch'en's troops

made a threatening advance, and Chiang is said to
have played a decisive role, or perhaps to have
played his role decisively, in recapturing certain
strategic positions and stabilizing the fluid military front. What his views or plans were when
Shen rebelled openly against the Kuomintang and
captured Shaokuan in early June is not known. We
do know, however, that on June 16, in the wake of
Shen's revolt, Sun appointed Chiang as chief-of-
staff to the Generalissimo's Field Headquarters.
Differences of opinion concerning military strategy must have arisen following this appointment,
for three weeks later Chiang considered resign-
ing from his new post on account of "misunderstanding and jealously." Finally, on July 12 he
resigned "in anger" and two days later left for
Chekiang.[194]

Upon his departure Chiang left behind a letter for his influential friend Yang Shu-k'an giving vent to his strong views on many issues. He
expressed deep dissatisfaction with Hsü Ch'ung-
chih's conduct of military affairs and with Liao
Chung-k'ai's leadership as governor of Kwangtung,
which province, he declared, "as things stand now,
cannot be regarded as the source of power for our
party." Under these circumstances, Chiang described himself as so "shaken up mentally" that he
could neither rest peacefully at night nor contain his passions in daily intercourse with his
colleagues. "If I do not leave Kwangtung now,"
he wrote in anger and anguish, "then all the comrades will be offended by me, thus doing irrepa-
rable damage to my personal relationships without
being of any benefit to the public cause." Chiang
noted that his departure had nothing to do with
the strength of his enemies; of them he was un-
afraid. What distressed him was the problem of
dealing with friends, or establishing a team of

compatible comrades. He added: "In my opinion,
it is more difficult to deal with the people within than those without. . . . During the three
months of my stay in Kwangtung, I was increasingly
distressed at the utter lack of purpose and discipline in my personal life and even more so at the
complete absence of vigor and achievement within
our party. If I return to Kwangtung [now, objective circumstances are such that] I will not
be able to control my despicable habit of violence and will even lose the good will of all my
friends." Chiang noted further that he "did not
have the natural gifts to be a staff officer" and
might better serve in a military post that allowed
him "to act summarily without interference from
anyone." For the moment, he would prefer to be
assigned to a mission of investigation to Russia,
for "in my opinion there is nothing to which I can
contribute" in China. If such an assignment could
not be brought about, then "I will be left with no
alternative but to take the negative step of at-
tending to my personal affairs and well-being."[195]
This letter, expressing a compelling desire to
visit Soviet Russia and to be given a command assignment, must certainly have been brought to the
immediate attention of Sun.

In view of political developments in Canton
at this time, it may be suggested that Chiang's
threat to leave the party unless his demands were
met was closely related to the emerging Kuomintang-Soviet collaboration and the attendant reallo-
cation of political and military influence in
Kwangtung. For nearly half a year since the party
declaration and the Sun-Joffe Manifesto of January
1923, discussions must have been continuing on
several levels within the Kuomintang on the subject of party reform and military reorganization.

87

On January 24 Chiang, then living as a private
citizen in Shanghai, is said to have received a
telegram from Ku Ying-fen, Li Chi-shen, Ch'en
K'o-yü, and Teng Yen-ta in Hong Kong, stating that
the "long-hoped-for party army" could not be realized unless Chiang were present in the south.[196]
Now, in June-July, having served as Sun's personal chief-of-staff, Chiang must have known something of the nature of anticipated Soviet assistance in matériel, personnel, and party reorganization.[197] His actions may therefore be construed as a decisive move to take advantage of
this unique opportunity to play an important role
in the programming and management of the forthcoming military aid. At any rate, his demands
produced the desired result. On August 5, with
Sun's authorization, he met with Maring, Chang
Chi, Wang Ching-wei, and Lin Yeh-ming in Shanghai
to discuss "the composition, etc. of the mission
to Russia."[198] Eleven days later Chiang left for
the Soviet Union with Shen Ting-i, Chang T'ai-lei,
and Wang Teng-yün, traveling via Japan and Harbin
and arriving in Moscow on September 2.[199] The
nature of Chiang's mission was described in Sun's
letter, dated September 17, to Soviet ambassador
Leo Karakhan in Peking:

> What follows is rigidly <u>confidential</u>.
> Some weeks ago I sent identical letters
> to Comrade Lenin, Tchitcherin, and Trotsky
> introducing General Chiang Kai-shek, who is
> my chief of staff and confidential agent.
> I have dispatched him to Moscow to discuss
> ways and means whereby our friends there
> can assist me in my work in this country.
> In particular, General Chiang is to take
> up with your government and military ex-
> perts a proposal for military action by my

forces in and about the regions lying
to the Northwest of Peking and beyond.
General Chiang is fully empowered to act
in my behalf.[200]

Chiang's departure from Moscow on November
29 was predictably sudden and unexpected. He
later explained to Sun that, while he had planned
to stay abroad for five or ten years (meaning an
extended period of time), news of Sun's unsuccess-
ful eastern expedition against Ch'en Chiung-ming
in August-November had so affected him that he
had decided to leave for Kwangtung immediately in
order to be of service to Sun, in total disregard
for his personal difficulties in the Kwangtung
environment.[201] Yet when he arrived in Shanghai
on December 15, he embarked for his home in Chekiang instead of for Kwangtung to make his report. Hu Han-min, Wang Ching-wei, Liao Chung-
k'ai, Lin Yeh-ming, and Ch'en Kuo-fu dutifully
went to his cabin to bid him farewell and to implore him "to return soon to Shanghai to deal with
party affairs."[202]

Chiang had probably calculated that the
unique experience and knowledge he had acquired
on his mission to Russia had made him indispensable to the Kuomintang, and he was stubborn and
"extreme" enough to make use of this fact to
strengthen his position within the party before
agreeing to proceed to Canton. Basically he was
concerned with two questions. First, there was
the broader issue of the power structure within
the Kuomintang and the attendant issue of the
governorship of Kwangtung. In Chiang's opinion,
the post should be taken from Liao Chung-k'ai,
whom he had criticized as inept at the time of his
last resignation, and given to Yang Shu-k'an, a
friend of his and of Chang Ching-chiang, although

Chiang had once disparaged him as being "too lazy" and "not worth the bother." Placing Yang in that key position would doubtless have improved the political atmosphere in Kwangtung from Chiang's point of view. Then, there was the more immediate and personally more imperative issue of his own role in the projected military academy. How much influence, for instance, would Liao and the recently arrived Borodin have in the academy? What authority would Chiang himself have?

Addressing themselves to the same questions, Liao, Hu Han-min, and Wang Ching-wei sent a joint telegram to Chiang on December 26. They advised him that Yang's assumption of the post of governor of Kwangtung required further consideration and in any event it "would not be necessary" for Chiang to postpone his trip to Shanghai until after the appointment had been announced. Additionally, they promised him "full responsibility" for the military academy, the organization of which, they continued, "cannot proceed without your proposals."[203] Chiang, however, wanted more specific assurances, and specifically he wanted to be able to make decisions, not merely proposals. Thus, on the 28th Liao wired him, possibly in response to his letters of the 23rd and 24th, that the dean of the academy would not be named until after Chiang had assumed office. Liao himself had been designated head of the academy's Political Department on the recommendation of Borodin, but he assured Chiang that he was prepared to resign in favor of Tai Chi-t'ao, and Chiang should therefore proceed to Canton without further delay so as not to make the entire affair appear a mere "plaything." Even Chang Ching-chiang grew impatient and telegraphed Chiang: "What am I to do now (nai-ho)? In my personal opinion you should not delay any longer." On the 30th Chiang, still in Chekiang, received a cable from Sun asking him to go quickly to Canton "to report all matters and make plans for Sino-Soviet cooperation."[204]

Having extracted concessions to the greatest possible degree and feeling also the pressure of events, Chiang left Shanghai for Kwangtung on January 16.[205] This was perhaps the latest possible date on which he could have embarked and arrived in Canton before the First National Congress of the Kuomintang was convened. It is also likely that his recalcitrance, so out of proportion to his importance within the party, had something to do with his exclusion from the Congress and from the higher councils of the party. Chiang is reported to have said of his own role at the Congress: "I was nominated to be a member of the Central Supervisory Committee, but my nomination was strongly opposed by our late Leader . . . out of consideration for [my] own good. For once having participated in the central party organization, there would be no opportunity to engage concretely in lower level activities."[206] But in the course of the Congress, Chiang did receive the appointment as chairman of the Preparatory Committee of the Military Academy on the 24th, and his friend Yang was indeed made governor of Kwangtung on the 29th.[207]

On February 3 Chiang was reappointed to the party's Military Council. But on the 21st he abruptly resigned as chairman of the Preparatory Committee and left for Chekiang.[208] What transpired, according to an informed student of Kuomintang military history, was that at a Preparatory Committee meeting on February 6, "Chiang and the Soviet advisers differed substantially on important points concerning the curriculum and management of the academy." Chiang, "indignant at Soviet objec-

tions to his plans" and unable to exercise full
authority as he would have it, tendered his resignation.[208] Years later Chiang explained that he
had resigned "at the end of the Congress" because
he had discovered in the course of the convention
that the Chinese Communists had "tried to increase their own importance by playing up Soviet
Russia," that some Kuomintang members "had been
swayed by Communist doctrines," and that as a
consequence he had been "full of misgivings regarding our Party's ability to carry out the task
entrusted to it by Dr. Sun."[209]

More revealing, however, was Chiang's long
letter of March 2 to Sun, in which he explained
in considerable detail his concern over the character and direction of political developments in
Kwangtung as well as the role he would wish to
assume within the Kuomintang. The letter was
frank, direct, and demanding to the point of arrogance, openly professing his conservative ideological and political orientation, and poignantly
expressive of an agonized soul desirous of both
personal power and public service, but not at the
expense of disturbing his own delicate psychological balance. He explained first that he had enjoyed the confidence neither of the party nor of
his superiors during his month-long stay in Kwangtung. For this estrangement he accepted partial
responsibility: "It happened that during the
month in Kwangtung, I was daily as restless as if
I were sitting on a mat full of nails. I was ab-
sentminded and careless, and aimless in my actions. I really don't know why I was so driven."
But while "base" and "stubborn," he protested, he
was also "loyal and sincere." And while he had
not proven himself in the performance of his duties during the preceding month, he had, "in my
opinion," a contribution to make to the party if

92

only he had the confidence of the comrades and were allowed to exercise his best judgments in discharging his responsibilities. Unfortunately, owing to political circumstances unrelated to his personal shortcomings, he had experienced "jealousy," "alienation," and factional strife within the party.

Chiang then brought up the matter that must have been foremost in his mind, namely, the question of "new influences" in the party. The Kuomintang, he observed, was passing through a transitional stage in its growth. However significant the "new influences," hitherto an unproven factor, might turn out to be in the future, the party must not forsake the "system" constructed through years of experience. "If the party has no system," he asked, "then why do we have a party? Indeed, there can be no party [without a system]. Wherein, if I may ask, lies the system of our party today? Is there really a central, undergirding force that can sustain it in each and every circumstance?" Within Sun's entourage there were many self-servers and power-seekers, he went on, but there was none who would give his utmost to serve the nation, the party, and Sun. Those whom Sun considered able and loyal were in fact mere opportunists and sycophants, and none among his followers could equal Ch'en Ch'i-mei and Chiang himself in their readiness to stand by Sun through thick and thin. How many, Chiang queried, were by Sun's side during Ch'en Chiung-ming's rebellion of 1922? Now that Sun had "sternly ordered" him to return to Kwangtung, Chiang said he would start his journey within a few days "to receive instruction," implying that he had not agreed to resume his post as chairman of the Preparatory Committee but that he was going to hear what Sun had to say. Chiang, however, had something urgent to say about his own role and he proceeded to make clear his position. He could not direct the academy without concerning himself with broader political and military questions, he announced, and would follow the saying, "Stay if compatible, leave if not compatible." He also declared that he would personally subscribe to China's traditional moral principles regardless of their current acceptability.

Arguing that the first requirement of the Kuomintang was the consolidation of its position in Kwangtung, not the formation of unstable alliances with neighboring provinces, he volunteered a few suggestions concerning personnel matters. He expressed his respect for Hu Han-min's knowledge, capacity, and moral rectitude and thought that, despite his many limitations, he would do well as governor of Kwangtung (a suggestion presumably offered as a compromise to replace Yang Shu-k'an, who had been appointed governor to succeed Liao Chung-k'ai at Chiang's insistence and was to be succeeded in turn by Liao in June, against Chiang's recommendation). Furthermore, Hsü Ch'ung-chih would be well suited to be commander-in-chief in Kwangtung but should not be entrusted with full authority (presumably he was not to be given the power once enjoyed by Ch'en Chiung-ming). Then Chiang raised in very personal terms the question of his own working relationship with Sun: "Do you not expect me to serve you in the same way you were served by Ch'en Ch'i-mei? [If so,] I dare to expect, in turn, that you trust me in the same way he trusted me. In your relationship with me today, do you really repose deep trust in me or do you not?"[210]

In the ensuing weeks Chiang maintained a steady communication with party leaders through

94

letters and telegrams. In a letter of March 14 to Liao Chung-k'ai he bluntly questioned the administrative ability of Liao, Tsou Lu, and Sun K'o, dismissed the "sincerity" of the Soviets in cooperating with the Kuomintang, and stressed the importance of bringing order to Kwangtung politics and rationalizing its administration. Moreover, he urged faithful party members to disagree with Sun Yat-sen if need be: "Spiritually and historically speaking, Mr. Sun's task has succeeded; but the effective implementation of this task at the present time is the responsibility of all of us and not that of Mr. Sun alone. We ought not simply to acquiesce and let matters drift, nor should we allow him to insist on his own opinions at the expense of the integrity of his comrades."[211] On the 25th he wrote to Hu Han-min and Wang Ching-wei and gave a surprisingly frank character portrayal of himself, on account of which, he said, he had followed the principle of "stay if compatible, leave if not compatible." He added that if in their opinion he must engage in public affairs, then they should create an environment in which he could work with peace of mind and over a long period.[212] On the 27th he wrote to four members of the Preparatory Committee --Wang Po-ling, Lin Chen-hsiung, Teng Yen-ta, and Yü Fei-p'eng--objecting to the change of the school term from six months to one year: "If the military academy is still to be established, then the rules and regulations which I decided upon, such as school term, curriculum, stipends, and admission policy, should be adhered to and need not be changed. . . . Do your duties and refrain from having too many opinions."[213] In a telegram to Liao on the 30th Chiang inquired as to financial arrangements for the academy and wanted to make certain that no difficulties existed in funding.[214] Liao replied in exasperation and with a sarcastic tone: "As to funds for the military academy, I will not ask about disbursements and you will not ask about their source. There is no lack of funds, and [you] can proceed to administer with peace of mind."[215]

Having received sufficient assurances concerning finances and appointment of personnel in reference to Hu Han-min, Yang Shu-k'an, Liao Chung-k'ai, Hsü Ch'ung-chih, Yang Hsi-yen, and Teng Tse-ju,[216] Chiang left Shanghai on April 14 and reported to Sun in Canton on the 21st.[217] On May 3 he was appointed commandant of the Whampoa Military Academy and chief-of-staff to the Kwangtung Army under the command of Hsü Ch'ung-chih.[218] Commenting on Chiang's relationship with the Soviet advisers at this time, one historian has said said that the "Russians, impressed by Chiang's assertiveness, and under orders from Galen and Borodin, temporarily limited their demands."[219] Thus, with Sun's support to the degree it was given and with a "suitable environment" to the extent it was possible, Chiang was sufficiently satisfied in his new posts to stay on. As commandant of the academy he was, as nearly as circumstances would permit, his own master; as chief-of-staff of the Kwangtung Army he was able to retain a sense of involvement in action. From this dual position as administrator-officer, he was to build the foundations of personal power and, eventually, to become President-Generalissimo of the nation.[220] Chiang's indebtedness to Sun for his political ascent cannot be overstressed.

Differences continued to exist between Sun and Chiang, however. During the next six months, until Sun's departure for Peking on November 13, Chiang was to disagree with Sun on many issues and even to disobey orders in several instances. They differed, for example, on the disposition of the rebellious Merchant Corps.[221] After confiscating the Corps' arms shipment for use by the Whampoa cadets, Chiang, in contravention of Sun's orders, refused to return the weapons seized and remarked brusquely: "If you [the Merchant Corps] have the ability, come and attack Whampoa; otherwise, don't talk about it." Their disagreement over this issue must have been a factor in influencing Chiang's formal though not final resignation as commandant of the Whampoa Academy on September 16.[222]

In early October dissent between Chiang and Sun arose over the composition of the Revolutionary Committee to be established for the purpose of crisis control. Against Borodin's advice, Chiang insisted that "on no account should Hu Han-min and Wang Ching-wei be excluded from the roster; otherwise it would be best to postpone its formation." Sun responded that henceforth the Soviet Union must be accepted as the revolutionary model. Since Hu Han-min did not share this belief, he "should naturally be excluded" from the Committee. Wang Ching-wei, he went on, was "really not a Russian-oriented revolutionary and might well be excluded." Like Hu, Wang was by nature a compromiser and unsuited for assignments requiring "thorough-going solutions." The Revolutionary Committee's functions, Sun emphasized, required the willpower "to cut the Gordian knot" and could not brook the "indecisiveness of dragging through mud and water." Impatient with the delay probably caused by Chiang's obstructive tactics, Sun told him that the Revolutionary Committee must be "inaugurated immediately."[223]

In another instance, Sun wrote to Chiang on October 8 castigating him for his failure to apply

to Whampoa the Soviet-inspired military organizational system Sun had personally drafted. His
disgust with Chiang's recalcitrance was evident
in his statement that the rejection of his plan
was a clear indication of the tradition-bound
mentality of those "Japanese-trained cadets and
Paoting officers who know very little and comprehend even less (i-chih pan-chieh) and who are totally ignorant of the general international situation."[224] Moreover, their disagreement over the
Second Northern Expedition which Sun had launched
on September 18 ran so deep that Chiang in fact
disobeyed Sun's direct orders to evacuate the
Whampoa and indeed requested the recall of Whampoa cadets from front line duties.[225]

Disagreements and disobedience notwithstanding, Chiang's basic loyalty to Sun was not shaken,
nor does it appear to have been questioned by Sun.
Thus, on July 7 Chiang was appointed commander of
the strategic Ch'angchow Fortress that overlooked
the approaches to Canton and Whampoa; on July 11
he was reappointed to the Military Council; on
July 15 he was named chairman of the Preparatory
Committee for the Military Training of All Armies;
on August 28 he was made one of the seven commis-
sioners of the revenue-producing Bureau of Rice
Control; on October 13 he became director of the
Training Board of Kwangtung Army Headquarters; on
October 14 he was given authority over various
military units in Canton to deal with the renewed
Merchant Corps crisis; and on November 11 he re-
ceived appointment as military secretary of the
newly created Military Department of the party's
Central Executive Committee to serve under Hsü
Ch'ung-chih.[226]

No suggestion is intended that Chiang would
necessarily have been given more important assign-

ments or entrusted with the primary responsibility
for nation-building had Sun lived longer to pre-
side over a more careful distribution of power
among the leading party personalities. With few
exceptions, all of the positions named above had
to do with the military. We may indeed deduce
from the inner logic of Chiang's personality that
had Sun lived to work with him over a longer period of time, differences between them would have
multiplied and intensified. Chiang, persuaded of
his own "sincerity," "integrity," "impartiality,"
and ability to judge issues on the merits of the
case, might have come to insist that Sun had out-
lived his usefulness, that the task of nation-
building was the "responsibility of all of us and
not that of Mr. Sun alone." And in a not impossible showdown between them, Chiang the soldier-
politician might have been no match for Sun the
unifier-inspirer.[227] What is suggested is this:
During his last years Sun included Chiang in the
periodic dispensation of power, which made Chiang
a man to be reckoned with; elevated him from the
military to the political plane by naming him to
the Revolutionary Committee, which testified to
Sun's recognition of his ability in crisis situations; and, out of both recognition and necessity,
appointed him commandant of the party's military
academy, which provided Chiang with the foundation
on which to build his own edifice of power in the
rapid succession of actual and simulated national
crises that followed Sun's death.[228]

When Sun departed for Peking on November 13
in desperate pursuit of that ever elusive dream of
peace for China, he stopped over at the Whampoa
Academy for three hours to review the future party
army of the Kuomintang.[229] Never lacking in hope
and ever striving to build public morale,[230] he
exclaimed in Chiang's presence: "Alas! The cadets

99

of this academy, enduring hardship and making strenuous efforts as they do, will surely be able to carry on my life's purpose and realize the party's principles. I can die now [in peace]."231 While this expression of enthusiasm gave no exclusive stamp of approval to Whampoa as the sole architect of a new China, Chiang perceived it differently. Sun had meant to say, as he interpreted it to the cadets in a speech on March 27, 1925, that "responsibility for the implementation of the Three People's Principles I have advocated will have to rest with the cadets of the Whampoa Military Academy. Man cannot escape death, but he can find fulfillment in death. The undaunted spirit I witness today in the officers and men at Whampoa can fulfill my life's purpose. If death should visit me now, I can die in peace."232 On the basis of this dialogue between the young officer who harbored great ambitions and the dying leader who dreamt great dreams, Chiang, as the commander-in-chief of the Northern Expeditionary Army and chairman of the Military Council, could say in February 1928: "Whampoa was personally created by Mr. Sun. It is his only legacy."233

Looking backward across the terrain he had traversed and forward over the heights of power yet to be conquered, Chiang had reason to focus his thoughts on the academy and to be grateful to Sun for the opportunities that the modern army offered him. Sun, in search of politico-military talents, had recruited Chiang into the inner circles of the Kuomintang and made him commandant of a professional, universalistic, and instrumental organization. Chiang, in search of power-qua-service, seized the opportunity with characteristic "extremeness" in self-regard and "rudeness" to conventions and utilized the military as an instrument to achieve personal political power in

a transitional China that demanded "clear-cut"
if not always "fundamental" solutions.[234]

VI. CONCLUSION

From this study several broad conclusions
may be drawn.

Psychologically, Chiang from his childhood
constructed a number of strong ego defense mechanisms against an experientially hostile world.
They were to become a powerful mental wall behind
which the rejected boy could withdraw in isolation, the better to preserve the stability of his
personality or to re-stabilize a personality
threatened with collapse. Given the environment
that surrounded him, it is understandable that in
erecting such a wall he should magnify the self
that stood defiant on one side and at the same
time reduce the perceived magnitude of the masses
that stood amorphous on the other. In Chiang's
case, however, there was an apparent unreality in
the balancing act between the in-group, which was
eventually reduced to one plus his family, and
the out-group of the whole-minus-one. And Chiang's
awareness of this unreality in all likelihood con-
tributed to his violent outbursts in early 1921
and eventually to the culmination and resolution
in 1921-23 of his prolonged identity crisis.[235]
This crisis, lasting for over fifteen years, was
volcanic, but Chiang emerged from it a "complete
man," having established the identity of his personality by making a life-long career decision,
by committing himself to a self-selected role
responsive both to his basic personality requirements and to the psychosocial milieu of the Chinese political stage, and by transforming the unreality of psychological isolation into a goal-
directed reality in which his "glorious stature"
stood in triumphant counterpoise to the "formless" and "soundless" humanity around him.

We might suggest that this identity crisis was not a simple case of megalomaniacal paroxysm. Rather, the cataclysmic nature of this experience may be construed as the result of the spilling over of his identity crisis into the integrity crisis which, according to one authority on human development, normally comes during the last years of the life cycle and which, when resolved, impels the possessor of "integrity" to perceive that "all human integrity stands or falls with the one style of integrity of which he partakes." The condensation of the much delayed identity crisis and the precocious integrity crisis in Chiang's life explains why he suffered from emotional disturbance to an extraordinary degree. At any rate, our evidence indicates a successful resolution of his identity crisis, by dint of which Chiang was able to overcome his psychological aberrations in a transitional society that was (and still is) anything but "normal."236 If a function of modern psychiatry is to accept a person as he is and proceed therefrom to establish a new set of self-other relationships in order that the person in question can reenter society with maximal productive capabilities, Chiang achieved this objective through rigidly regulated self-analysis and through a religiously cultivated faith in himself.

Chiang's continued involvement in society was undoubtedly impelled by the value-attitudes he had developed at home and in school. His mother, like most mothers in recorded history, had a great capacity for interweaving ideals with reality and instilled in him the idea of service to mankind, of relatedness to this world. She also hoped, "anxiously" we are told, "that I should make a name for myself." At school Chiang learned that one could become famous as a rebel, like the Taiping leaders, or as a model, like Tseng Kuo-fan. But whether he acted in his destructive role as a rebel—the "red-faced general" against school authority, the dare-to-die leader in the anti-Manchu uprising, or the self-appointed revolutionary dispenser of justice in the liquidation of T'ao Ch'eng-chang—or in his constructive role in later years as statesman-model and paragon of virtues, involvement in action was a trait ideologically sanctioned by parental example at home, by the classics taught at school, as well as by the temperamental requirements of his own psychological makeup. Involvement in action was in his nature; involvement in the name of service was a value implanted in his nature. Thus, as he erected the mental wall that rendered him immune to the "irrelevancies" and "bores" of this world, he was attempting not to remove himself from this world but to relate himself more effectively to it.[237]

This, in a large measure, accounted for the strength of character that was to commend Chiang to party leaders. He had the will power to cut the Gordian knot and was not in the habit of "dragging through mud and water." He was prepared to become involved in the service of the party and the nation, but only if he was entitled to that no-nonsense straightforwardness, "stay if compatible; leave if not compatible." If the party desired his service, he laid down but a single, if open-ended, condition, namely, that he be given a suitable environment in which his psychological equilibrium would not be disturbed in order that he could bring about "clear-cut and fundamental solutions" to the nation's manifold problems. And he made this demand with disarming frankness, having recognized through self-analysis his person-

104

ality defects and his psychological requirements as a productive public servant. This self-diagnosis was disclosed not only to friends such as Chang Ching-chiang and Tai Chi-t'ao, but also to party leaders such as Liao Chung-k'ai, Hu Han-min, and Wang Ching-wei.

Party leaders, despite their cognizance of his personality traits, desired his services. Obviously, they believed that Chiang's assets outweighed his liabilities, and perhaps they also persuaded themselves that their collective political acumen would be more than adequate to contain his ambitions and to outmaneuver his brusque challenges. At that particular juncture in China's political development, certain otherwise undesirable qualities of Chiang's would be of significant utility to the Kuomintang movement. Chiang was known for his unstable and peripatetic public career, but that was why he, unlike Ch'en Chiung-ming and Hsü Ch'ung-chih, had no personal power base and why he became increasingly valuable to the Kuomintang as the party's orientation became increasingly universalistic. He did not have the wide-ranging scholarly attainments of men like Chu Chih-hsin and Chü Cheng, but this lack was compensated for by the specific and disciplined training of a soldier whose skills were in great demand following the Kuomintang reorganization of 1923-24. He alienated himself from the out-group and was even critical of his superiors, including Sun Yat-sen, but for precisely this reason he was during those early years largely untethered by traditional affective bonds and able to strike out with a refreshingly secular mode of operation. He was terribly self-regarding, but that was the quality that sustained him in his stand against accepted standards and enabled him to exercise his best judgment in attempting new achievement criteria in public administration. He was impatient, as Sun noted, but he was capable of resolute action, a quality that gave him a place on Sun's Revolutionary Committee. He was intolerant of sluggishness and therefore was able to quickly shape the Whampoa cadets into an effective fighting force and serve as their model at a critical moment in the party's history.

Finally, while psychologically he set himself against the outside world, a condition which conceivably distorted his perception of reality, he also had an unusual capacity to rise above himself into the "spatial void" and look at himself with an extraordinary degree of detachment and objectivity. Thus, he was never so programmatically extremist as to pit himself against the entire out-group or build a pyramidal power structure with himself alone at the apex. Rather, he would observe the human drama from his Olympian height, calculate in terms of systemic requirements and policy priorities, and make optimal utilization of existing groups for the achievement of his desired ends. That was why Chiang, unlike Sun's other military followers, was not unfavorably disposed toward the party's new united front policy and, despite his ingrained conservatism, was able to work reasonably satisfactorily with Borodin and the Chinese Communists for a period of about three years, from 1924 to 1926. And it should be added that while Chiang was opportunistic in his public pronouncements during these years of Kuomintang-Communist alliance, he did not hide his conservative bent and the Communist leadership knew him as he basically was.[238] The Chinese Communist Party and the Comintern, like the Kuomintang, needed him for the qualities and qualifications he possessed and found it not impossible to work with him in a relationship of mutual exploitation.

106

In conclusion it may be said that the qualities Chiang possessed and the leadership he was
able to provide were situationally required by
China in the transitional period of the 1920s.
His recruitment into a responsible military position within the party establishes a prima facie
correspondence between the political qualities
manifested in Chiang's personality and the functional requirements of the Chinese nation at a
time of rapid transformation. In this sense he
was a "born" leader in the political development
of twentieth century China.[239]

Heretofore studies of Chiang Kai-shek,
whether scholarly or popular, adulatory or denunciatory, have been guided by established, if
not always "culture-bound," standards of social
criticism and have given us strong views and new
insights into a complex man from different per-
spectives. The primary task of social criticism
is, of course, to appraise, adjudge, and criticize
and, at its best, to bring out in the most analy-
tic terms the differences between the principles,
policies, programs, and practices of the object
of study on the one hand, and the social values,
norms, goals, and processes implicitly or explicit-
ly endorsed by the author on the other. Not con-
sciously an exercise in social criticism, this
study is designed as an exploratory "clinical" investigation of a political man within his own
sociopolitical context. With this approach it has
been possible to say that the Chiang constructed
in this case study was a natural phenomenon.
Whether the historical Chiang was a necessary factor in modern China is a question that cannot be
answered with any degree of precision, owing both
to the information gaps under which we labor and
to the intellectual blind spots we cannot yet

107

overcome with our present state of theoretical
sophistication. Despite these limitations, however, recent advances in the social sciences war-
rant another attempt to gain new understanding of
Chiang from a developmental perspective. This
study represents such an attempt. From it we
perceive a political man who, given the personality tensions within himself and the societal tensions within the Chinese nation, deserves an "im-
partial" hearing such as we may be able to provide.

NOTES

[1]Huang Chi-lu, "Kuo-fu shih-shih ch'ien hou,"
in Cheng Chao et al., Sun Chung-shan hsien-sheng
kan-i lu (Taipei: Wen-hsing shu-tien, 1965),
p. 154.

[2]S.I. Hsiung, The Life of Chiang Kai-shek
(London: Peter Davies, 1948), pp. 290-91. Li
Tsung-jen recalled: "As soon as the service
started, Mr. Chiang suddenly placed his hand upon
the coffin and wept bitterly, as if he would
really destroy himself in his grief." Li Tsung-
jen, "The Reminiscences of General Li Tsung-jen,"
as recorded by T.K. Tong, unpublished manuscript,
dated December 1, 1964, Chinese Oral History Project, East Asian Institute, Columbia University,
Part 2, p. 27 (7). I am grateful to Professor C.
Martin Wilbur for permission to use this document.

The American minister to China, J.V.A. Mac-
Murray, reported to the secretary of state on
August 6, 1928: "General Chiang read a report of
the steps leading to the successful conclusion of
the northern expedition, which was followed by
three minutes' silent prayer for those killed in
the revolution. General Chiang was so overcome
with emotion during the ceremony that he collapsed
before the coffin of Sun Yat-sen sobbing, whereupon Marshal Feng [Yü-hsiang] lifted him up and
supported him away." Papers Relating to the
Foreign Relations of the United States, 1928, vol.
2, p. 161.

[3]Cf. Erik H. Erikson, Childhood and Society
(New York: W.W. Norton & Co., 1964); Erik H. Erikson, Young Man Luther: A Study in Psychoanalysis

109

and History (New York: W.W. Norton & Co., 1958); Erik H. Erikson, Identity: Youth and Crisis (New York: W.W. Norton & Co., 1968).

[4]Cf. Robert C. Tucker, "The Dictator and Totalitarianism," World Politics, vol. 17, no. 4 (July 1965), pp. 555-83; Fred I. Greenstein, "The Impact of Personality on Politics: An Attempt to Clear Away Underbrush," American Political Science Review, vol. 61, no. 3 (September 1967), pp. 629-41. Greenstein's article has been further developed in his Personality and Politics: Problems of Evidence, Influence, and Conceptualization (Chicago: Markham Publishing Co., 1969) and in his shorter study by the same title in Seymour Martin Lipset, ed., Politics and the Social Sciences (New York: Oxford University Press, 1969), pp. 163-206.

J. David Singer argues that "the cultural properties of any subnational, national or extranational system may be described in a strictly aggregative fashion, by observing the distribution and configuration of individual psychological properties." See his "Man and World Politics: The Psycho-Cultural Interface," Journal of Social Issues, vol. 24, no. 3 (July 1968), pp. 143-44.

Neil J. Smelser cautions that "we do not at present have the methodological capacity to argue causally from a mixture of aggregated states of individual members of a system to a global characteristic of the system." See his "Personality and the Explanation of Political Phenomena at the Social-System Level: A Methodological Statement," Journal of Social Issues, vol. 24, no. 3 (July 1968, p. 123.

[5]Cf. Harold D. Lasswell, Psychopathology and Politics (Chicago: University of Chicago Press, 1930); Harold D. Lasswell, Power and Personality (New York: W.W. Norton & Co., 1948); T.W. Adorno et al., The Authoritarian Personality (New York: Harper & Row, 1950); Lucian W. Pye, Politics, Personality, and Nation-Building: Burma's Search for Identity (New Haven: Yale University Press, 1962).

[6]Chen Pu-lai and Tang Cheng-chu, eds., Chronology of President Chiang Kai-shek (Taipei: China Cultural Service, 1954), p. 1.

[7]Mao Ssu-ch'eng, Min-kuo shih-wu nien i-ch'ien chih Chiang Chieh-shih hsien-sheng (Hong Kong: Lung-men shu-tien, November 1965), 1:1 ts'e, pp. 1a-2a; hereafter referred to as Mao (A). This is a photocopy of the edition said to have been published in October 1936, the date of Mao's postscript.

[8]Chéou-kang Sié, President Chiang Kai-shek: His Childhood and Youth (Taipei: China Cultural Service, [1954]), p. 9.

[9]Hollington K. Tong, Chiang Kai-shek: Soldier and Statesman (Shanghai: China Publishing Co., 1937), vol. 1, pp. 2-3. Tong was himself a native of Chekiang.

[10]For the inscription, see Mao (A), 1:1 ts'e, pp. 8a-12a; Hsiung, pp. 17-21. Also see Chu Chih-hsin, Chu Chih-hsin chi (Shanghai: Min-chih shu-chü, February 1928), vol. 2, pp. 615-16.

[11]Mao (A), 1:1 ts'e, pp. 5b-7b; Hsiung, pp. 7-9.

[12] Mao (A), 1:3 ts'e, pp. 2a-7b; Hsiung, pp. 10-15.

[13] For the eulogy, dated June 25, 1921, see Mao (A), 3 ts'e, pp. 77b-83a; Hsiung, pp. 22-27; Chiang Chung-cheng, "Hsien-pi Wang t'ai-fu-jen shih-lüeh," in Chiang tsung-t'ung yen-lun hui-pien, vol. 24 (Taipei: Cheng-chung shu-chü, October 1, 1956), pp. 63-65. For the elegy, dated June 15, 1921, see Mao (A), 3 ts'e, pp. 75b-77b; Chiang Chung-cheng, "K'u mu wen," in Yen-lun hui-pien, vol. 24, pp. 141-42. Also see his "Tz'u an chi," in Mao (A), 5 ts'e, pp. 74b-76b, under the December 17, 1923 entry; and in Chiang Chung-cheng, Tzu-fan lu (n.p., [1931?]), 1:6, 517-18, erroneously dated winter of 1922. Unless otherwise noted, the following account of Chiang's family is based on the eulogy.

[14] Chu Chih-hsin's eulogy for Chiang's father, in Mao (A), 1:1 ts'e, p. 11a-b.

[15] Ibid., p. 11b.

[16] Mao (A), 1:3 ts'e, p. 13b. In another version of Chiang's "diary," the date is given as 1909; see Mao Ssu-ch'eng, Min-kuo shih-wu nien i-ch'ien chih Chiang Chieh-shih hsien-sheng, ed. by Ch'en Pu-lei, vol. 1 (n.p., [1948?]), p. 24; hereafter referred to as Mao (B). I am indebted to Professor C. Martin Wilbur for the use of his personal copy of the Mao-Ch'en version.

[17] Mao (A), 2 ts'e, p. 14b.

[18] Chiang's eulogy for his maternal grandfather, in ibid., 1:3 ts'e, p. 5b.

[19] Ibid., 1:1 ts'e, p. 4b.

112

[20]Ibid., p. 5a.

[21]Ibid., 1:2 ts'e, p. 5a.

[22]Ibid., p. 2b; Chen and Tang, pp. 2-3.

[23]Chiang Chung-cheng, "Wang ti Jui-ch'ing ai-chuang," April 10, 1918, in Tzu fan lu, 1:6, p. 439. According to Chiang, his eldest son Ching-kuo was, upon Ts'ai-yü's instructions, formally entered into the family's geneological table as the adopted son of Jui-ch'ing; ibid., pp. 438, 441.

[24]Mao (A), 1:2 ts'e, pp. 4b-5a.

[25]Wen-hua li-chin she, Chiang wei-yüan-chang chuan (Shanghai: Tso-hsin shu-tien, May 1937), p. 21.

[26]The material in this paragraph is drawn from Mao (A), 1:1 ts'e, pp. 4a-5b, 8a; 1:2 ts'e, passim.

[27]Hsiung, p. 37.

[28]Mao (A), 1:2 ts'e, p. 7b. The translation is from Hsiung, p. 41.

[29]Gabriel A. Almond and G. Bingham Powell, Jr., Comparative Politics: A Developmental Approach (Boston: Little, Brown & Co., 1966), pp. 64-67. For two recent general studies of political socialization, see Richard E. Dawson and Kenneth Prewitt, Political Socialization (Boston: Little, Brown & Co., 1969); Kenneth P. Langton, Political Socialization (New York: Oxford Univer-

sity Press, 1969). Also see Herbert H. Hyman, Political Socialization: A Study in the Psychology of Political Behavior (Glencoe: The Free Press, 1959). For the concept of political culture, see Gabriel A. Almond, "Comparative Political Systems," Journal of Politics, vol. 18, no. 3 (August 1956), pp. 391-409; Gabriel A. Almond and Sidney Verba, The Civic Culture: Political Attitudes and Democracy in Five Nations (Princeton: Princeton University Press, 1963), especially chap. 1, "An Approach to Political Culture"; Lucian W. Pye and Sidney Verba, eds., Political Culture and Political Development (Princeton: Princeton University Press, 1965), especially Verba's concluding chapter, "Comparative Political Culture." Also see Coleman's Introduction in James S. Coleman, ed., Education and Political Development (Princeton: Princeton University Press, 1965), pp. 3-32. For a pioneering study of the Chinese political culture, see Lucian W. Pye, The Spirit of Chinese Politics: A Psychocultural Study of the Authority Crisis in Political Development (Cambridge: The M.I.T. Press, 1968).

[30]The information in this paragraph is taken from Mao (A), 1:1 ts'e, pp. 5b, 8a; 1:2 ts'e, pp. 1b-2b, 4a, 5b, 6b, 7b; 3 ts'e, p. 97b; Mao (B), vol. 1, pp. 3-13; Hsiung, pp. 33-50, which provides the indented translation. Also see Mao Ssu-ch'eng, "Min-kuo yüan-nien ch'ien chih Chiang Chieh-shih hsien-sheng," in Teng Wen-i, ed., Wei-ta ti Chiang chu-hsi (Kuo-fang-pu hsin-wen-chü, 1946), pp. 44-51; hereafter referred to as Mao (C). Cf. Chiang Hsing-te, "Chu-hsi chih sheng-p'ing," ibid., pp. 56-68; Chiang Hsing-te, "Chiang chu-hsi ti tu-shu sheng-huo," in Li Hsü, ed., Liu-shih nien lai ti Chung-kuo yü Chiang chu-hsi (Nanking: Pa-t'i

shu-chü, 1946), pp. 139-41; T'ao Pai-ch'uan, ed., Chiang chu-hsi ti sheng-huo ho sheng-huo-kuan (Chungking: Chung-chou ch'u-pan-she, 1944), pp. 75-76; Wu I-chou, Chiang tsung-t'ung hsing-i (Cheng-chung shu-chü, 1954), pp. 11, 26-30.

[31]The information in this and the following paragraphs is taken from Mao (B), vol. 1, pp. 14-19. It generally follows the account in Mao (C), pp. 48-51, but differs on several points from Mao (A), 1:2 ts'e, pp. 8a-10a and 1:3 ts'e. Also see Chen and Tang, pp. 4-6.

The determining factor in influencing me to accept the Mao (B) version over the Mao (A) version is the information, given in both accounts that Chiang received his military training certificate from the Shimbu Gakkō on November 25 of Meiji 43, or 1910. Mao (B) presents it under the 1910 entry, as does Mao (C), while Mao (A) erroneously gives the same information in the 1909 entry. I might add that I am not completely convinced of the accuracy of the Mao (B) version in every detail. My reservations concerning its biographical accuracy, however, do not compromise its usefulness for the present study, which is to investigate the psychological history and political socialization of Chiang. In fact, Mao (A) would do quite well for this purpose also. Still, in the interest of biographical clarity, I shall point to discrepancies between the two versions and comment on them when deemed helpful.

Mao (A) puts Chiang at the Phoenix Mountain School in 1903, when he created the student disturbance, and at the Golden Arrow School in 1904.

[32]On the fiftieth anniversary of his birth, Chiang wrote about the alleged persecution of "my

115

family" as follows: "It will be remembered that
the then Manchu regime was in its most corrupt
state. The degenerated gentry and corrupt officials had made it a habit to abuse and maltreat
the people. My family, solitary and without influence, became at once the target of such in-
sults and maltreatment. From time to time usu-
rious taxes and unjust public service were forced
upon us, and once we were publicly insulted before
the court. To our regret and sorrow none of our
relatives and kinsmen was stirred from his apathy."
Hsiung, Appendix 2, "Some Reflections on my Fiftieth Birthday," p. 374; Chiang Chung-cheng, "Pao-
kuo yü ssu-ch'in," October 31, 1936, in Yen-lun
hui-pien, vol. 24, pp. 68-69. Also see Mao (B),
vol. 1, p. 18.

[33]Tong, Soldier and Statesman, vol. 1, p.
vii. Mao (A) gives February-April 1905 as the
period when Chiang attended the Dragon River Middle School.

[34]About ego identity, Erikson has this to
say: "It is the accrued experience of the ego's
ability to integrate all identifications with the
vicissitudes of the libido, with the aptitudes developed out of endowment, and with the opportunities offered in social roles. The sense of ego
identity, then, is the accrued confidence that the
inner sameness and continuity prepared in the past
are matched by the sameness and continuity of
one's meaning for others, as evidenced in the tan-
gible promise of a 'career.'" Erikson, Childhood
and Society, pp. 261-62. Elsewhere, Erikson elab-
orates on the process of identity formation:

　　Identity formation . . . begins where the
　usefulness of identification ends. It arises
　from the selective repudiation and mutual as-

similation of childhood identifications and
their absorption in a new configuration,
which, in turn, is dependent on the process by
which a society (often through subsocieties)
identifies the young individual, recognizing
him as somebody who had to become the way he
is and who, being the way he is, is taken for
granted. . . .

The final identity, then, as fixed at the
end of adolescence, is superordinated to any
single identification with individuals of the
past: it includes all significant identifications, but it also alters them in order to
make a unique and reasonably coherent whole
of them. . . .

It is the ego's function to integrate the
psychosexual and psychosocial aspects on a giv-
en level of development and at the same time to
integrate the relation of newly added identity
elements with those already in existence--that
is, to bridge the inescapable discontinuities
between different levels of personality development. . . . From the genetic point of view
. . . the process of identity formation emerges
as an evolving configuration--a configuration
which is gradually established by successive
ego syntheses and resyntheses throughout childhood. It is a configuration gradually integrat-
ing constitutional givens, idiosyncratic libid-
inal needs, favored capacities, significant
identifications, effective defenses, successful
sublimations, and consistent roles.

Erikson, Identity, pp. 159-63. The identity crisis
constitutes the fifth, puberty-adolescence stage of
the eight-stage life cycle, according to Erikson.
It grapples with past and present conflicts as it
also sets the stage for future crises. "At a given
age, a human being, by dint of his physical, intel-

117

lectual and emotional growth, becomes ready and
eager to face a new life task, that is, a set of
choices and tests which are in some traditional
way prescribed and prepared for him by his society's structure. A new life task presents a crisis
whose outcome can be a successful graduation, or
alternatively, an impairment of the life cycle
which will aggravate future crises." Erikson,
Young Man Luther, p. 254.

[35]Mao (A), 1:3 ts'e, pp. 1b-2a, states that
Chiang left for Japan in mid-1905 and made the acquaintance of Ch'en Ch'i-mei in Tokyo later that
year. This version suggests that "he was there"
on July 30, 1905 when Sun Yat-sen and several
scores of revolutionary leaders held a preliminary
meeting to discuss the formation of a new party,
and on August 20 when the T'ung-meng-hui (the
United League, a precursor of the Kuomintang) was
formally inaugurated. Cf. Lo Chia-lun, Kuo-fu
nien-p'u erh kao (n.p., n.d.), vol. 1, pp. 177,
179. The story, however, has at least three draw-
backs. First, no reference can be found to indicate that Chiang was in fact present at either
the July 30 meeting, attended by some seventy persons, or the August 20 meeting, attended by over
three hundred persons. Second, Ch'en Ch'i-mei's
first journey to Japan did not take place until
mid-1906. Ho Chung-hsiao, Ch'en Ying-shih hsien-
sheng nien-p'u (Shanghai: China Cultural Service,
April 1946), p. 10; Shao Yüan-ch'ung, "Hsing-
chuang," in ibid., p. 76; P'an Kung-chan, Ch'en
Ch'i-mei (Taipei: Sheng-li ch'u-pan kung-ssu,
1954), p. 13. Third, if Chiang indeed took the
journey in May 1905, it would have meant that he
left home only one month after the death of his
maternal grandmother who, he wrote, "often shared

our house and always our sorrow." Chiang's mother "wept bitterly" over the loss and exclaimed several times, "I am already a widow and now my mother dies, so what is there worth living for? The only reason that I should wait a little while is that my son is not grown up yet." Cf. Chiang's eulogy for his maternal grandmother, in Mao (A), 1:3 ts'e, pp. 2b, 4a; Hsiung, pp. 10-11. We would expect that Chiang, however restless he may have been at this time, would not have insisted on leaving his mother under such circumstances, nor would his mother have been likely to subsidize his journey at this time had he insisted.

Hollington K. Tong's account is rather confusing on this point: he gives 1905 in two instances and 1906 in a third. Tong, Soldier and Statesman, vol. 1, pp. vii, xxiii, 13.

Schiffrin accepts 1905 as the year of Chiang's first trip to Japan. See Harold Z. Schiffrin, Sun Yat-sen and the Origins of the Chinese Revolution (Berkeley: University of California Press, 1968), p. 258, note 13, citing as his source Hsiung, pp. 49-50, which is based on Mao (A).

[36] Chiang, "Pao-kuo yü ssu-ch'in," p. 69; Hsiung, Appendix 2, p. 374. Hsiung's translation, used here, does not include the bracketed passage.

[37] Professor Hackett gives the following figures for Chinese students in Japan at the time Chiang ventured abroad to study: 1904--1,200-1,400; 1905--2,641 as of July 1, 3,000 as of July 15, and 8,000 in December; 1906--7,000 in January, 10,000 in July, and 13,000 in September; June 1907--8,000; July 1908--4,896. Roger F. Hackett, "Chinese Students in Japan, 1900-1910," Papers on China

(Cambridge: Committee on International and Regional Studies, Harvard University), vol. 3, May 1949, p. 142.

Professor Y.C. Wang has described the Chinese students in Japan at this time as follows: "The number of Chinese students there jumped from 1,300 in 1904, to 2,400 in January of 1905, and to 15,000 in September of 1906. But most of these students were interested only in acquiring titles and not in actual study. According to a survey made by the Board of Education, approximately 60 per cent of the Chinese students were enrolled in short-term training courses, 30 per cent in elementary courses, 3 to 4 per cent in high schools, and only 1 per cent in universities. The remaining 5 to 6 per cent were perpetually transferring from one school to another." See Y.C. Wang, Chinese Intellectuals and the West, 1872-1949 (Chapel Hill: University of North Carolina Press, 1966), p. 64. Also see Robert Scalapino, "Prelude to Marxism: The Chinese Student Movement in Japan, 1900-1910," in Albert Feuerwerker, Rhoads Murphey, and Mary C. Wright, eds., Approaches to Modern Chinese History (Berkeley: University of California Press, 1967), p. 192.

[38] It has been suggested that Chiang's decision to pursue a military career was influenced by his admiration for Yo Fei. See H.H. Chang, Chiang Kai-shek: Asia's Man of Destiny (Garden City, N.Y.: Doubleday Doran & Co., 1944), pp. 44-45.

[39] A series of regulations concerning military education in Japan, drawn up in 1904, required government endorsement in order to undertake study of military science. Y.C. Wang, Chinese Intellectuals and the West, p. 67.

[40] Kuo T'ing-i, Chin-tai Chung-kuo shih-shih jih-chih, Ch'ing-chi (Taipei: Cheng-chung shu-chü, 1963), vol. 2, p. 1268. Also see Ralph L. Powell, The Rise of Chinese Military Power, 1895-1912 (Princeton: Princeton University Press, 1955), pp. 182-83.

[41] Mao (B), vol. 1, p. 21; Lo Chia-lun, Liu-shih nien lai chih Chung-kuo Kuo-min-tang yü Chung-kuo (Central Executive Committee of the Kuomintang, Fourth Section, Commission for Compiling Historical Documents of the Party, November 1954), p. 23.

[42] Mao (B), vol. 1, pp. 22-25.

[43] Quoting Hsiung, p. 50.

[44] Mao (B), vol. 1, p. 19; Chen and Tang, p. 5. Chiang's eulogy for Ch'en Ch'i-mei, written in 1916, mentions their warm friendship of "ten years since ting-wei." Ting-wei is generally referred to as 1907, as is the case with the "diary." More precisely, it falls between February 13, 1907 and February 1, 1908. For the eulogy, see Mao (A), 1:5 ts'e, pp. 17a-19a; also in Ho Chung-hsiao, ed., Ch'en Ying-shih hsien-sheng chi-nien ch'üan-chi (n.p., [1930?]), 1:4, 13a-b. For calendrical conversion, see Hsieh Chung-san and Ou-yang I, comps., Liang-ch'ien nien Chung-Hsi li tui-chao piao (Hong Kong: The Commercial Press, 1961), p. 380.

I must admit that I continue to be somewhat puzzled by this statement of Chiang's. Given his professed feelings toward Ch'en, it would appear that he ought to know when their warm relationship began. In fact, this assumption nearly led me to accept the original Mao (A) version, which states that Chiang made his first trip to Japan in May

121

1905, returned to China that winter, was sent to Japan as a government-sponsored cadet in early 1907, and was recommended for party membership by Ch'en Ch'i-mei sometime during 1907. However, a number of other considerations lead me to accept, in the absence of additional verifiable biographical data, the general validity of the revised Mao (B) version. If the correctness of the ting-wei reference is in doubt, one might offer the following as explanations: (1) Chiang has the habit of giving quantitative data in round figures, and the reference to the "ten years since ting-wei" may be simply another example of that tendency; (2) the close relationship between Ch'en and Chiang did not develop until sometime after the republican revolution, and no special event in Japan came to Chiang's mind in 1916 to mark the beginning of that relationship; and (3) Chiang has been known to give inexact dates and incorrect information.

[45]There is a wealth of contradictory data on Chiang's induction into the party, of which the following are a few. Mao (B), vol. 1, p. 23, cites 1908, while Mao (A), 1:3 ts'e, p. 10, gives 1907. Lo Chia-lun (Kuo-fu nien-p'u, vol. 1, p. 238), citing Mao (A) instead of Mao (B), accepts 1907. Fu Ch'i-hsüeh gives 1908, as do Chen and Tang. See Fu Ch'i-hsüeh, Kuo-fu Sun Chung-shan hsien-sheng chuan (Taipei: Preparatory Committee of Various Circles in the Republic of China to Commemorate the Hundredth Anniversary of the Birth of the Founding Father, November 1965), p. 424; Chen and Tang, p. 5. Huang Chi-lu, in a letter to the author dated March 13, 1969, explains that the year 1908 "should be correct." To add to the confusion, 1906 is cited by C.W.H. Young, New Life for Kiangsi (Shanghai, 1935), p. 144. Hollington

K. Tong (Soldier and Statesman, vol. 1, pp. 14,
16) simply states that Chiang "arrived in Japan
in 1907" as a cadet and that he subsequently "became a member of the Tungmenghui."

An incomplete membership roster of the T'ung-
meng-hui for the years 1905-06, with the exception
of one person whose membership is dated 1907, is
given in Lo Chia-lun, ed., Ke-ming wen-hsien,
vol. 2 (Taichung: Commission for Compiling Historical Documents of the Party, Central Executive
Committee of the Kuomintang, December 1958), pp.
158-217. Also see Feng Tzu-yu, Chung-hua min-kuo
k'ai-kuo ch'ien ko-ming shih hsü-pien (Shanghai:
China Cultural Service, August 1946), vol. 1, pp.
127ff. The roster does not include Chiang nor,
for that matter, Ch'en Ch'i-mei. It is generally
agreed, however, that Ch'en did join the party in
late 1906 or early 1907 (ping-wu year, January 25,
1906-February 12, 1907). See Feng, Ke-ming shih
hsü-pien, vol. 1, p. 73; Ho, Ch'en Ying-shih nien-
p'u, p. 10; P'an, p. 13; Shao Yüan-ch'ung, Ch'en
Ying-shih hsien-sheng ke-ming hsiao-shih (Shanghai:
Min-chih shu-chü, [1925?]), p. 4; Shao, "Hsing-
chuang," p. 76.

[46]Ibid., p. 77. Ch'en's own stature in the
party and among the revolutionaries was not recognized until about 1911. According to Chang Chi,
he was told in 1943 by Yü Yu-jen: "Ch'en Ch'i-mei
was very unlucky at first in Shanghai. [I] introduced [him] to Chang Ching-chiang [in 1908?], but
Ching-chiang blamed [me] for introducing an inap-
propriate person. There was no one but myself who
would help Ch'i-mei." Chang Chi, Chang P'u-ch'üan
hsien-sheng ch'üan-chi (Taipei: Chung-yang wen-wu
kung-ying-she, October 1951), vol. 1, p. 362.

[47]Ho, Ch'en Ying-shih ch'üan-chi, published
in or about 1930, makes no mention of a meeting between Chiang and Sun in Japan. His Ch'en Ying-shih
nien-p'u, completed in 1944 and published in 1946,
refers almost casually, on p. 13, to Ch'en introducing Chiang to Sun during the ting-wei year
(1907-08); however, according to Mao (B), Chiang
was not in Japan at that time. Chen and Tang, p.
5, says that "Chiang met Dr. Sun Yat-sen for the
first time" in Japan in 1909; this is obviously an
error, for Sun was away from Japan during the entire period; cf. Lo, Kuo-fu nien-p'u, vol. 1, pp.
262-70. Lo (ibid., p. 285) states that the two
met during the fifth moon in 1910 (June 7-July 6);
Lo, who in this study usually supports his data
with documentation, offers none for this significant piece of information. Kao Yin-tsu explains
that Sun arrived in Yokohama on June 15, 1910 and
"received" Chiang during this short stay in Japan.
See Kao Yin-tsu, Kuo-fu nien-piao chien-pien ([Tai-
pei?]: Chung-hua min-kuo ta-shih-chi pien-i-she,
November 1966), p. 19. Hsiung (pp. 50-51, 55)
makes the guess that 1907 was a "more probable
date" than 1905.

Tong (Soldier and Statesman, vol. 1, p. 16)
quotes Sun as saying during their alleged first
meeting, "That man will be the hero of our Revolution: we need just such a man in our revolutionary
movement."

Another 1937 publication declared: "The
Chairman, in cadet uniform, stood proudly and attentively before Mr. Sun. Mr. Sun gazed at him
for a good while and exclaimed: 'Is this Chiang
Kai-shek? I am so glad to meet you.' That evening they discussed politics, frankly and freely,
deep into the night. After this the Chairman be-

came a key figure in the T'ung-meng-hui and Mr. Sun
always consulted him before making any plans."
Chin Ch'eng, ed., Chiang Chung-cheng ch'üan-chi,
vol. 2 (Shanghai: Min-tsu ch'u-pan-she, June 1937),
Appendix, "Chiang Chieh-shih hsien-sheng chuan-
lüeh" (A Summary Biography of Mr. Chiang Kai-
shek), p. 2. In 1945 Teng (Wei-ta ti Chiang chu-
hsi, p. 14) had Sun remark: "This cadet officer
will most assuredly be an extraordinary talent in
our party." Fu Ch'i-hsüeh, like Chiang's "diary,"
is silent on this point. For one of the most
apocryphal accounts, see Sié, pp. 70-72.

Howard L. Boorman, ed. Biographical Dictionary
of Republican China, vol. 1 (New York: Columbia
University Press, 1967), p. 164, provides this account: "Although some Kuomintang sources state
that Ch'en Ch'i-mei introduced Chiang Kai-shek to
Sun Yat-sen, this story seems to be apocryphal, for
Sun had been ordered to leave Japan in the spring
of 1908." It is unfortunate that this generally
acceptable comment seems to be contradicted on
pp. 319-20 by what appears to be a reference to Lo
Chia-lun: "Chen introduced Chiang to Sun Yat-sen
when Sun returned briefly to Japan from Honolulu
in 1910."

[48]Mao (A), 1:3 ts'e, p. 13a; Mao (C), pp. 50-
51. Mao (B), vol. 1, p. 24, gives the same passage in the 1909 entry, possibly due to careless
textual rearrangement during the revision. In
1941 Chiang said that he read the book at the age
of 18 sui, that is, in 1904; Chiang Chung-cheng,
"Che-hsüeh yü chiao-yü tui-yü ch'ing-nien ti kuan-
hsi," July 9-10, 1941, in Yen-lun hui-pien, vol.
15, p. 281.

[49]Mao (B), vol. 1, pp. 23-24.

[50]Ibid., p. 27; and Mao (A), 1:4 ts'e, p. la.
After this point in time, the two versions, with
few exceptions, coincide.

[51]Mao (B), vol. 1, p. 24.

[52]For the well-known Lasswellian formulation
that a politician is one who displaces private
motives on public objects in the name of collec-
tive advantage, see his Psychopathology and Poli-
tics, p. 124; Power and Personality, p. 38; and
Politics: Who Gets What, When, How (Cleveland:
World Publishing Co., 1958), pp. 21, 133. Cf.
Alexander L. George, "Power as a Compensatory
Value for Political Leaders," Journal of Social
Issues, vol. 24, no. 3 (July 1968), pp. 29-49.

[53]T'ang Leang-li, The Inner History of the
Chinese Revolution (London: George Routledge &
Sons, 1930), pp. 252-53. Chang Ching-chiang, a
virtual cripple wearing tinted glasses in later
years, did seem to have a "sinister" look about
him; but T'ang's words and tone could probably be
best construed as a disapproving reference to
Chang's old-fashioned manipulative politics and
to the success that old politics in his seasoned
hand could bring.

Far more critical than T'ang is Kuo-min chiu-
kuo-hui, Chiang Chieh-shih Ch'en Chi-t'ang mai-
kuo yang-min i-p'ieh (n.p., 1933), p. 9. A technique in character assassination used by Chiang's
opponents is to call into question the validity of
his genealogy and the legitimacy of his birth (and
that of Soong Mei-ling). See ibid., pp. 10-11;
T'ang-jen (pseud.), Chin-ling ch'un-meng, with a
preface by Fei I-min (Hong Kong: Yang Yung, [1955],
1966), vol. 1, pp. 1-41; Ch'en Shao-chiao (pseud.),

Hei wang lu (Hong Kong: Chih-ch'eng ch'u-pan-she, 1965), pp. 212-13.

[54]Cheng Tsung-hsi, Wang An-tsiang, and Wang I-ting, General Chiang Kai-shek: The Builder of New China, with an Introduction by Chengting T. Wang and a Preface by Wang Chung-hui (Shanghai: The Commercial Press, 1929), pp. 10-13.

[55]J. Leighton Stuart, Fifty Years in China: The Memoirs of John Leighton Stuart (New York: Random House, 1954), p. 118. Also see Ishimaru Tōta, Chiang Chieh-shih chuan, trans. by Shih Lo-ying (Shanghai: Kuang-hua ch'u-pan-she, 1937), p. 32.

[56]Mao (A), 1:4 ts'e, pp. 1a-2a; "Chung-kuo ta-shih chi" (Major Events in China), Tung-fang tsa-chih, vol. 8, no. 9 (November 15, 1911), p. 9; Shen I-yün, I-yün hui-i, vol. 1 (Taipei: Biographical Literature, Inc., April 1, 1968), pp. 57, 72; Hsü T'ang, Hsin-hai kan-ssu-t'uan yüan-ch'i yü Hu chün-shih ke-ming shih-lüeh, extracted in Chung-hua min-kuo k'ai-kuo wu-shih nien wen-hsien pien-tsuan wei-yüan-hui, ed., Chung-hua min-kuo k'ai-kuo wu-shih nien wen-hsien, 2d series, vol. 3, Hsin-hai ke-ming yü min-kuo chien-yüan, p. 368.

[57]Mao (A), 1:4 ts'e, pp. 1b-2b; Chiang Chung-cheng, "Wei Hang-chou kuang-fu chi fu Ku Tzu-ts'ai shu," in ibid., vol. 4, Ko-sheng kuang-fu, p. 145. and also in Chiang, Yen-lun hui-pien, vol. 24, pp. 80-81; "Chung-kuo ta-shih chi" (Major Events in China), Tung-fang tsa-chih, vol. 8, no. 10 (April 1, 1912), p. 1; Lo, Kuo-fu nien-p'u, vol. 1, p. 349, citing Ch'u Fu-ch'eng, Che-chiang hsin-hai ke-ming chi-shih (A True Record of the 1911 Revolution in Chekiang), at the Kuomintang Archives;

Kuo, vol. 2, p. 1420; Shen, vol. 1, pp. 56-57, 63-65, citing Ko Chan-hou, Hsin-hai ke-ming yü Che-chiang (The 1911 Revolution and Chekiang); P'an, p. 31; Ho, Ch'en Ying-shih nien-p'u, pp. 19-20.

[58]Mao (A), 1:3 ts'e, p. 12a-b and 1:4 ts'e, pp. 2b-3a; Mao (B), vol. 1, pp. 23-24 and vol. 2, "Chiang Chieh-shih hsien-sheng nien-piao" (A Biographical Synopsis of Mr. Chiang Kai-shek), p. 7; Fu, pp. 134, 166; Feng Tzu-yu, Chung-hua min-kuo k'ai-kuo ch'ien ke-ming shih (Shanghai: China Cultural Service, [May 1944], January 1946), vol. 2, p. 156.

[59]Teng Wen-i, Chiang chu-hsi (Shanghai: Sheng-li ch'u-pan-she, 1945), p. 16. Teng's 1946 version merely states that Chiang "liquidated T'ao Ch'eng-chang"; Teng Wen-i, Chiang chu-hsi chuan-lüeh (Kuo-fang-pu hsin-wen-chü, 1946), p. 6. See Sié, pp. 91-92, for a different version.

Chiang is known to have personally killed the murder suspect in the death of Liao Chung-k'ai: "He killed one culprit, Ch'en Shun, on the spot"; Mao (A), 11 ts'e, p. 65b. Also see note 77 below.

[60]Mao (A), 1:4 ts'e, pp. 4b-5b.

[61]Ibid., 1:5 ts'e, pp. 1a-2b; Shao, "Hsing-chuang," p. 80; Shen, vol. 1, p. 86; Hu Ch'ü-fei, Tsung-li shih-lüeh (Shanghai: The Commercial Press, October 1937), p. 187; Ho, Ch'en Ying-shih nien-p'u, pp. 40-43. Ho (p. 48) states that Chiang accompanied Ch'en Ch'i-mei (not Chang Ching-chiang) to Ningpo in Chekiang (not Nanking) after the Shanghai debacle, failed to fan military defections, and "returned to Shanghai immediately."

[62]Upon Ch'en's death, Chiang wrote an eulogy
tracing Ch'en's activities back to 1913; Chiang
Chung-cheng, "Ch'en Ying-shih hsien-sheng kuei-
ch'ou hou chih ke-ming chi-hua chi shih-lüeh," in
Ho, Ch'en Ying-shih ch'üan-chi, 1:1, 24b-29b.
This eulogy also appears in Chiang, Yen-lun hui-
pien, vol. 24, pp. 31-36, bearing the date of May
26, 1916.

It is interesting to note that the pictorial
section of Ho, Ch'en Ying-shih ch'üan-chi, published in or around 1930, identifies Chou Jih-
hsüan, Ting Ching-liang, and Yü Chien-kuang as
"three comrades who were associated [with Ch'en]
day and night from the abortive uprising in 1913
to 1916." Chiang is not mentioned as being one of
them.

[63]Lo, Kuo-fu nien-p'u, vol. 1, p. 495, citing
the membership roster of the Chinese Revolutionary
Party. Also see Fu, p. 425.

[64]Mao (A), 1:5 ts'e, pp. 2b-5a; Lo, Kuo-fu
nien-p'u, vol. 1, p. 504, with Kuomintang Archives
documentation; P'an, p. 87; Ho, Ch'en Ying-shih
nien-p'u, p. 51; Hu, p. 196; Tsou Lu, Chung-kuo
Kuo-min-tang shih-kao (Taipei: The Commercial
Press, 1965), vol. 3, p. 991.

[65]Mao (A), 1:5 ts'e, pp. 5a-9b. Also see
Chiang, "Ch'en Ying-shih chih ke-ming chi-hua," p.
25a-b; Ho, Ch'en Ying-shih nien-p'u, pp. 49-51;
P'an, pp. 86-87; Lo, Kuo-fu nien-p'u, vol. 1, p.
497.

[66]Ibid., vol. 1, p. 536, citing Hsü's communi-
cation bearing a notation by Sun, and the Daily
Record of the Military Affairs Department of the
Chinese Revolutionary Party.

129

[67]Ibid., vol. 1, pp. 549, 551, 552, citing
guest books of the party's General Affairs Department.

[68]Mao (A), 1:5 ts'e, pp. 12a-14b; Chiang,
"Ch'en Ying-shih chih ke-ming chi-hua," p. 28a-b;
Shao Yüan-ch'ung, "Ch'ao-ho chan-yü shih-chi," in
Ho, Ch'en Ying-shih ch'üan-chi, 1:1, 29b-34b;
Lo, Kuo-fu nien-p'u, vol. 1, pp. 560-61; Lo, Liu-
shih nien lai chih Chung-kuo, p. 20; Tsou Lu, vol.
3, pp. 992-96; Ho, Ch'en Ying-shih nien-p'u, p. 66.
P'an, pp. 90-96. Also see Marius B. Jansen, The
Japanese and Sun Yat-sen (Cambridge: Harvard Uni-
versity Press, 1954), pp. 195-96, citing North
China Daily Herald, December 11, 1915, which reported disapprovingly the disturbances created by
"buccaneers" and "desperadoes." For the plan
drafted by Chiang, see Lo, Ke-ming wen-hsien, vol.
6, pp. 770-76. Chang Chi was wrong in identifying
Chiang as Ch'en's chief-of-staff; Chang Chi, Chang
P'u-ch'üan hsien-sheng ch'üan-chi pu-pien (Taipei:
Chung-yang wen-wu kung-ying-she, June 1952), p.
161. Ch'en's chief-of-staff was Wu Chung-hsin;
the marine commander was Yang Hu. For disciplin-
ary action proposed against the naval personnel
who had responded to the overtures of the revolutionaries, see "Chung-kuo ta-shih chi" (Major
Events in China), Tung-fang tsa-chih, vol. 13, no.
1 (January 1916), p. 8. After the death of Ch'en
in 1916, Chiang Kai-shek, Hsü Ch'ung-chih, Wu
Chung-hsin, Shao Yüan-ch'ung, and others petitioned
Sun Yat-sen to declare December 5, the day of the
Chao-ho incident, as a Memorial Day for Revolutionary Martyrs; Lo, Kuo-fu nien-p'u, vol. 2, p.
608.

[69]Mao (A), 1:5 ts'e, p. 16a-b. In his 1916
essay Chiang merely refers to the abortive at-

130

tempt to capture and hold the Kiangyin Fortress
in advance of a projected attack on the Kiangnan
Arsenal. There is no reference to his own role
in this uprising, but neither is Yang Hu mentioned; see Chiang, "Ch'en Ying-shih chih ke-ming
chi-hua," p. 29a. The following publications mention Yang but not Chiang: Ho Chung-hsiao, "Nien-
p'u ch'u-kao" (1930?), in Ho, Ch'en Ying-shih
ch'üan-chi, 1:1, 7b; Hu Ch'ü-fei, Tsung-li shih-
lüeh (1937), p. 199; Ho, Ch'en Ying-shih nien-p'u
(1946), p. 74; P'an (1954), p. 98.

Several publications, with varying degrees
of emphasis on this period, fail to mention
Chiang altogether in connection with the revolutionary episodes of the years 1911-16 discussed
herein. See, for example, Shao, Ch'en Ying-shih
hsiao-shih (1925?), pp. 8-18; Hua Lin-i, Chung-
kuo Kuo-min-tang shih, ed. by Ts'ai Yüan-p'ei
(Shanghai: The Commercial Press, June 1928), pp.
29-46; Chung-kuo Kuo-min-tang chung-yang chih-
hsing wei-yüan-hui Yüeh-Min ch'ü hsüan-ch'uan
chuan-yüan pan-kung-ch'u, ed., Kuo-fu Sun hsien-
sheng nien-p'u (n.p., [1939?]).

[70]Chiang said in 1964: "In the Kiangyin
Fortress Incident of 1916, and in the Sian Incident of 1936, I was struggling against danger
alone without any outside assistance in sight."
See Chiang Chung-cheng, "Director-General Chiang
Kai-shek's Message to Kuomintang Members on the
Seventieth Anniversary of the Party's Establishment," Chung-yang jih-pao, November 30, 1964, p. 1
(original text in English).

[71]Mao (A), 1:5 ts'e, pp. 16b-17a. Ch'en Kuo-
fu saw his uncle Ch'en Ch'i-mei in Chiang's residence on May 16. Ch'en Kuo-fu, in Ho, Ch'en Ying-

shih ch'üan-chi, 1:1, p. 57a-b, "Chuan-shu" (Biographical Notes).

[72]Mao (A), 1:5 ts'e, p. 19a-b; Chü Cheng, Mei-ch'uan p'u-chieh (privately distributed by Chang Ming, 1949), p. 23a-b; Lo, Kuo-fu nien-p'u, vol. 2, pp. 569, 575-76, 590, citing Chü Cheng, Chü Chüeh-sheng hsien-sheng ch'üan-chi (Collected Works of Mr. Chü Cheng), vol. 1, p. 51.

[73]See Sun Yat-sen's telegrams of June 10 and September 5, 1916 to Chü Cheng, in Sun Chung-shan, Kuo-fu ch'üan-shu, compiled by Chang Ch'i-yün (Taipei: Kuo-fang yen-chiu-yüan, 1960), pp. 665, 667.

[74]Mao (A), 1:5 ts'e, p. 19b.

[75]Ibid., 2 ts'e, pp. 1a-14a.

[76]Ibid., p. 19b.

[77]"Confidential" letter, November 29, 1926, C.E. Gauss, U.S. Consul General in Shanghai, to J.V.A. MacMurray, U.S. Minister to Peking (with copy to the Secretary of State), on the subject of the "Criminal Record of Chiang Kai-shek," U.S. National Archives, Records of the Department of State Relating to the Internal Affairs of China, 1910-29, Microfilm No. M-329, Roll No. 56. The full text of the letter reads as follows:

> Sir:
>
> The prominence of Chiang Kai Shek as leader of the Cantonese Government forces now penetrating the Yangtze Valley has apparently led into some inquiry as to his record.

I quote below for your confidential
information copy of a memorandum ob-
tained by a member of my staff from
the Intelligence Office of the Municipal Police of the International
Settlement at Shanghai.

The archives of the Municipal Police
contains no less than three warrants
for the arrest of one Tsiang Kya Zah
(蔣介石), otherwise written Chiang
Kai Shek, who seems beyond doubt to
be the General now in command of the
Southern forces. One of the warrants
issued at the instance of the Defense
Commissioner at Shanghai on July 22,
1914, charges Tsiang with crime in
Siau Soo Doo (小沙渡) district; the
second issued on October 13, 1917,
accuses him of being concerned in
the murder of a prominent Chinese
resident of the Settlement in 1910;
and a third, issued at the instance
of the Military Governor of Sunkiang
and Shanghai on July 25, 1918, al-
leges that Tsiang was concerned in
armed robbery at No. 1421 Seward
Road, on October 18, 1917.

I have the honor to be, Sir,
     Your obedient servant,

          C.E. Gauss
          American Consul General
          in charge

   Regarding the alleged murder in 1910, it will
be remembered that Chiang was in Japan from 1908
to 1911 except during the summers, when he returned to China "to help rescue the imprisoned

comrades." Considering the fact that this murder charge was not preferred against him until 1917, it is possible that it was confused with Chiang's assassination of T'ao Ch'eng-chang in early 1912. The 1914 "crime" had to do with Chiang's anti-Yüan activities in Shanghai in May-June. As for the armed robbery in 1917, which took place only a few weeks after Sun Yat-sen assumed his position as generalissimo of the Military Government in Canton on September 1, the best possible interpretation is that it was a dramatic act in support of a meagerly financed insurgent movement such as revolutionaries throughout the world have been known to commit.

The New York Times (November 14, 1926, p. 18) reported: "Those who recall events in Shanghai a decade ago remember that General Chiang Kai-shek, the present victorious Cantonese leader, is still under criminal indictment in this settlement for alleged armed robberies. . . ."

[78]Lo, Kuo-fu nien-p'u, vol. 2, p. 646, citing records of the Generalissimo's Headquarters.

[79]Mao (A), 2 ts'e, pp. 20a, 24a, 51a, 52a, 54a-b, 71b, 72a, 84a, 85b; 3 ts'e, pp. 2a, 2b, 4a, 5a, 10a, 24b, 61b, 62a, 74b, 92a, 93a-b, 98b; 4 ts'e, pp. 10b-11a.

[80]Ch'eng T'ien-fang, Ch'eng T'ien-fang tsao-nien hui-i lu (Taipei: Biographical Literature, Inc., October 1968), p. 39.

On his frequent visits to Sun's residence in Shanghai from 1917 to 1919, Chiang Monlin recalls that he came to know Hu Han-min, Chu Chih-hsin, Liao Chung-k'ai, Ch'en Shao-pai, Tai Chi-t'ao, Chang Chi, Chü Cheng, Lin Sen, and Tsou Lu; he

134

does not mention Chiang or Wang Ching-wei. See
Chiang Meng-lin, "Chui-i Chung-shan hsien-sheng,"
in Cheng Chao, p. 33.

[81]Sun, Kuo-fu ch'üan-shu, p. 775. Also see
Mao (A), 2 ts'e, pp. 86a-88a; Lo, Kuo-fu nien-p'u,
vol. 2, p. 716.

[82]Kuo-fang-pu ch'u-pan-she, ed., Wei-ta ti
Chiang chu-hsi (Hong Kong: Pai-ling-han, 1946),
p. 34.

[83]Mao (A), 2 ts'e, pp. 65a, 89a; 3 ts'e, pp.
la, 3a; 6 ts'e, p. 35a-b. Chiang had earlier had
an eye ailment, but that was in 1913 and was the
result, we are told, of reading the complete works
of Tseng Kuo-fan; ibid., 1:5 ts'e, pp. 2b-3a.

[84]Y.C. Wang, "Tu Yueh-sheng (1888-1951): A
Tentative Political Biography," Journal of Asian
Studies, vol. 26, no. 3 (May 1967), p. 437, cit-
ing two sources that refer to Chiang's employment
in a brokerage house: Harold R. Isaacs, The
Tragedy of the Chinese Revolution (Stanford,
1961), p. 81; and Ch'en Po-ta, Jen-min kung-ti
Chiang Chieh-shih (Peking, 1954), p. 5. Cf. Wu
Hsiang-hsiang, Min-kuo cheng-chih jen-wu (Taipei:
Wen-hsing shu-tien, 1966), vol. 2, pp. 126-27;
Boorman, vol. 1, pp. 75, 202, 321.

[85]For his battle plans relating to Fukien
and Chekiang, drafted in December 1917, presumably in his capacity as military counselor to
Sun, see Chiang, Tzu-fan lu, 1:1, 87-92. At the
request of Ch'en Chiung-ming, in January 1919 he
drafted a proposal for the construction of a can-
tonment large enough to accommodate one division;
for this plan, see ibid., 1:4, 274-79. He also

135

wrote "Fei-tu ts'ai-ping i," February 19, 1919,
ibid., pp. 24-26.

[86]The battle referred to took place in Fukien
in December 1918; Mao (A), 2 ts'e, pp. 58b-59a.
For his memoir of this battle, dated January 26,
1919, see *ibid.*, pp. 59b-64a; Tzu-fan lu, 1:2,
140-44. For Sun's telegram of December 13, 1918
urging Hsü Ch'ung-chih and Chiang Kai-shek not to
resign their commissions, see Sun, Kuo-fu ch'üan-
shu, p. 631.

[87]Mao (A), 3 ts'e, pp. 2b, 4b-5b.

[88]Chu, Chu Chih-hsin chi, vol. 2, p. 642.

[89]Mao (A), 3 ts'e, p. 6b.

[90]Ibid., pp. 9b-10a.

[91]Ibid., pp. 10a-12a.

[92]Ibid., pp. 17a-18a; Sun, Kuo-fu ch'üan-shu,
pp. 798-99; translation adapted from Hsiung, pp.
115-16.

It is perhaps relevant to note that Sun had
a higher opinion of Chu than he had of Chiang's
mentor Ch'en Ch'i-mei. Sun is reported to have
said: "Ch'en Ch'i-mei had revolutionary zeal and
courage but was lacking in knowledge and scholarship. Chu Chih-hsin had Ch'en's revolutionary
spirit, but his knowledge and scholarship sur-
passed that of Ch'en." [Tai] Chi-t'ao, "Huai Chu
Chih-hsin hsien-sheng," in Chu Chih-hsin, Chu
Chih-hsin wen-ch'ao, compiled by Shao Yüan-ch'ung
(Shanghai: Min-chih shu-chü, May 1927), p. 434.

[93]Adapted from Hsiung, p. 116.

[94] Mao (A), 3 ts'e, pp. 24b–29b. The letter appears on pp. 25b–26a; translation adapted from Hsiung, p. 117.

[95] Mao (A), 3 ts'e, p. 30a-b. For telegrams from Hu Han-min, Chang Ching-chiang, and Tai Chi-t'ao, dated November 11, 18, 20, and 24, see ibid., pp. 30b–32a. Also see Hu Han-min's communication to Sun, requesting the early return of Hsü Ch'ung-chih and Chiang; Lo, Kuo-fu nien-p'u vol. 2, p. 758, citing Kuomintang Archives.

[96] Mao (A), p. 32a-b. Chiang did not see his "very ill" mother until the 22nd and then only for one day, though it should be added that he "returned home" again from November 26 to December 2; ibid., pp. 32b–33b.

[97] Ibid., pp. 33a–34a.

[98] Ibid., pp. 42a-b; translation adapted from Hsiung, pp. 118-19.

[99] Mao (A), 3 ts'e, pp. 46b–48a; translation adapted from Hsiung, pp. 119–22. This letter also appears in Tai Chi-t'ao, Tai Chi-t'ao hsien-sheng wen-ts'un, comp. by Ch'en T'ien-hsi, vol. 4 (Taipei: Central Executive Committee of the Kuomintang, 1959), pp. 1481-82.

[100] Mao (A), 3 ts'e, pp. 42b–46b; translation adapted from Hsiung, pp. 122–24. This letter also appears as "Fu Tai Chi-t'ao shu," in Yen-lun hui-pien, vol. 24, pp. 102-03.

[101] Mao (A), 3 ts'e, pp. 48b–51a. It may be of interest to note that Chiang's first plan for a northern expedition, submitted to Sun on Septem-

137

ber 20, 1917, also envisaged a sea invasion from
the Yangtze River to the general area of Chinwangtao. Ibid., 2 ts'e, p. 8a.

[102] Ibid., 3 ts'e, pp. 51a-53a; Hsiung, p.
127; Chiang Chung-cheng, "Yü Chang Ching-chiang
shu," in Yen-lun hui-pien, vol. 24, p. 101.

Chou Jih-hsüan was from Chiang's native province of Chekiang and had been a close friend of
his since 1908. In 1918 Chiang had "contact" with
both Chang Ching-chiang and Chou in Shanghai before the latter's departure for Szechuan in October. Chou died in Chengtu in June 1919. Mao (B),
vol. 1, p. 23; Mao (A), 2 ts'e, pp. 19b, 65a,
73a-b; Chu Chih-hsin's letter of July 7, 1919 to
Chiang, in Chu, Chu Chih-hsin chi, vol. 2, pp.
641-42.

Like Chou, Shao Yüan-ch'ung was from Chekiang. The three Chekiangese had had a long-
standing association going back to the days of
Chiang's association with Ch'en Ch'i-mei. In
1915 they were part of a group that worked closely under Ch'en, the others being Wu Chung-hsin,
Yang Shu-k'an, Ting Ching-liang, and Yü Chien-
kuang. See Mao (B), 1:5 ts'e, p. 12b; Tsou Lu,
vol. 3, p. 993. However, the nature of the monetary transaction desired by Chiang is not known,
and I intend no suggestion that Shao knew anything
about Chiang's demands.

Chiang and Shao shared a common dislike for
Ch'en Chiung-ming, although Shao was far more ac-
commodating. During a mission in the fall of
1918 to investigate conditions prevailing in
Kwangtung and Fukien, Shao reported to Sun, who
was in Shanghai: "I have nothing to do here because Ch'en Chiung-ming has a very complex staff
under him. Moreover he has no organization.

Every functionary is directly responsible to the
commander-in-chief. Everything goes its own way;
there is no coordination. A newcomer [like me]
cannot help him at all. So I will wait until Hsü
Ch'ung-chih solves his problems at the front and
goes to the provincial capital, where I can help
him, as we suit each other better. At present I
am staying with Ch'en Chiung-ming temporarily.
If you have any instructions for Hsü Ch'ung-chih,
Chiang Kai-shek, or me, please have Chu Chih-hsin
write to me and I will pass them on." Mao (A), 2
ts'e, p. 56b; translation adapted from Hsiung, pp.
106-07. Shao was to be the only fatality among
Chiang's entourage during the Sian coup of 1936.

[103]Boorman, vol. 2, pp. 259-61; China Year
Book, 1929-30, p. 954; Tsou Lu, vol. 3, p. 1065.

[104]Tang Tsou, America's Failure in China,
1941-50 (Chicago: University of Chicago Press,
1963), pp. 122-23.

[105]Mao (A), 3 ts'e, pp. 53a-54b.

[106]Ibid., pp. 39a-41b.

[107]Ibid., pp. 54b-55a; Hsiung, p. 125.

[108]Mao (A), 3 ts'e, p. 61a-b.

[109]Ibid., pp. 57a-61a.

[110]Ibid., pp. 61b-62a.

[111]For the letter, see ibid., pp. 65b-69a;
Hsiung, pp. 132-34. The passage cited here is
from Mao (A), p. 69b, and Hsiung, p. 134. In this
letter Chiang also expressed his dissent over the

impending inauguration of Sun as constitutional
president, on the grounds that "the time is not
yet ripe, and our foundation is far from being
solid." He went on to refer to a confidential
talk he had had with Hsü Ch'ung-chih who, he
claimed, concurred in his views: "This is what
Hsü Ch'ung-chih said to me and for me only, and
in turn I say it to you, sir, and for you only,
and I trust you will not infer from this that Hsü
Ch'ung-chih is also one of the persons opposing
you."

[112] Mao (A), 3 ts'e, pp. 69b–74b.

[113] Ibid., pp. 74b–75a.

[114] Ibid., pp. 83a–93b; Hu Han-min, "Liu
yüeh shih-liu hui-ku," in Chung-kuo Kuo-min-tang
Kuang-tung sheng chih-hsing wei-yüan-hui, Sun ta-
tsung-t'ung Kuang-chou meng-nan shih-chou-nien
chi-nien chuan-k'an ([Canton], June 1932), p. 16.

[115] Mao (A), 3 ts'e, pp. 94b–100b; 4 ts'e,
p. 11a.

[116] Chiang's letter of February 1921 to Teng
K'eng, in ibid., pp. 64b–65a.

[117] Chiang's letter of January 10, 1921, to
Chang Ching-chiang, in ibid., p. 52a.

[118] Ibid., 1:4 ts'e, pp. 4b–5a. For studies
of and methodological comments on opinions and per-
sonality, see Gabriel A. Almond, The Appeals of
Communism (Princeton: Princeton University Press,
1954); M. Brewster Smith, Jerome S. Bruner, and
Robert W. White, Opinions and Personality (New
York: John Wiley & Sons, Inc., 1956); M. Brewster
Smith, "Opinions, Personality, and Political Be-

havior," American Political Science Review, vol.
52, no. 1 (March 1958), pp. 1-17; Alexander L.
George, "Comments on [M. Brewster Smith's] 'Opinions, Personality, and Political Behavior,'"
ibid., pp. 18-26; Robert E. Lane, Political Ideology: Why the American Common Man Believes What
He Does (New York: The Free Press, 1962); M.
Brewster Smith, "A Map for the Analysis of Personality and Politics," Journal of Social Issues,
vol. 24, no. 3 (July 1968), pp. 15-28; Greenstein, Personality and Politics (1969); Robert E.
Lane, Political Thinking and Consciousness: The
Private Life of the Political Mind (Chicago:
Markham Publishing Co., 1969).

[119]Chiang Chung-cheng, "Chün-sheng tsa-
chih fa-k'an-tz'u," 1912, in Tzu-fan lu, 1:5,
413-17.

[120]Chiang Chung-cheng, "Chün-cheng t'ung-i
wen-t'i," 1912, in Tzu-fan lu, 1:5, 345-55.

[121]Chiang Chung-cheng, "Ke-ming chan hou
chün-cheng chih ching-ying," July 1912, in Tzu-
fan lu, 1:5, 319-45.

[122]Chiang Chung-cheng, "Meng-Ts'ang wen-
t'i chih ken-pen chieh-chüeh," [October] 1912, in
Tzu-fan lu, 1:5, 356-67.

[123]Chiang Chung-cheng, "Pa-erh-kan chan-
chü ying-hsiang yü Chung-kuo yü lieh-kuo chih wai-
chiao," [November?] 1912, in Tzu-fan lu, 1:5,
368-76.

[124]Chiang Chung-cheng, "Cheng Meng tso-
chan ch'u-i," December 1912, in Tzu-fan lu, 1:1,
48-80.

141

[125]Mao (A), 1:5 ts'e, pp. 2b–3a, 10b–11a; Chiang Hsing-te, "Chiang chu-hsi ti tu-shu shenghuo," p. 144.

[126]Mao (A), 2 ts'e, p. 65a–b.

[127]Ibid., pp. 66a, 89a–90a; 3 ts'e, p. 34a–b.

[128]Ibid., 2 ts'e, pp. 65b–66a.

[129]Ibid., p. 89a–b.

[130]Ibid., 3 ts'e, pp. 34b–36a. These letters also appear in Chiang, Yen-lun hui-pien, vol. 24, p. 118. Cf. Chiang Ching-kuo, Fu-chung chih-yüan (Taipei: Kuo-fang-pu yin-chih-ch'ang, 1960), section 1, p. 93.

[131]Mao (A), 3 ts'e, pp. 97a–100b.

[132]Ibid., p. 101a–b.

[133]He read Sherlock Holmes for relaxation on board the warship Yung-feng in 1922; ibid., 4 ts'e, p. 69a. More serious materials on psychology, statistics, sociology, economics, world geography, the First World War, the Russo–Japanese War, the Franco-Prussian War, and the military exploits of Napoleon were included in his long reading list for 1924; ibid., 8 ts'e, pp. 79b–81a. On April 25, 1926, during the hectic period between the March 20 coup and the Second Plenary Session of the Second Central Executive Committee in May, he read the leftist journal Hsin ch'ing-nien (not La Jeunesse); ibid., 15 ts'e, p. 48a; cf. Chow Tse-tsung, The May Fourth Movement: Intellectual Revolution in Modern China (Cambridge: Harvard

University Press, 1960), pp. 44-45, note d. He read a history of the Communist Party of the Soviet Union on July 21, and <u>Hsiang-tao chou-pao</u> (Guide Weekly) in August, in the midst of preparations for the Northern Expedition; Mao (A), 16 ts'e, pp. 42b, 121a-b. In November 1936, when Chiang was in Loyang making plans for a decisive campaign against the Communists, "Ho Ts'ui-lien [Franklin L. Ho] received orders to remain in Loyang and to discourse daily with Mr. Chiang on the financial systems of England, France, and America." Ch'en Pu-lei, <u>Ch'en Pu-lei hui-i lu</u> (Taipei: Biographical Literature, Inc., January 1967), pp. 115-16. H.H. Chang reported from firsthand knowledge: "[Chiang] keeps a secretarial staff busy bringing him information about new books and publications about which he desires to know something. But the fact remains that Chiang's whole background and training are so thoroughly Chinese, and he draws so heavily on Chinese learning and scholarship that it is impossible to conceive of him apart from this Chinese milieu." H.H. Chang, pp. 220-21.

[134]Concerning Chiang's acting according to his instincts, I am reminded of the comment he made on October 8, 1926: "The key to military and political affairs lies in the functioning of the cerebellum (<u>hsiao-nao tso-yung</u>)." Mao (A), 18 ts'e, p. 34b.

[135]<u>Ibid.</u>, 5 ts'e, pp. 79a-80b.

[136]<u>Ibid.</u>, 1:5 ts'e, p. 20a. Sun "heard" that it was her fiftieth birthday; she was in fact 53 <u>sui</u> in 1916.

The revised version of the "diary," edited by Ch'en Pu-lei, reports that the occasion was Chiang's thirtieth birthday on October 31, 1916 and that "Sun personally arrived at [Chiang's] residence to offer his congratulations" and "presented the tablet inscribed 'expertise in child rearing' as his greetings to Chiang's mother." Mao (B), vol. 1, p. 505. This may well be correct; in any event, Chiang had returned to Shanghai from Shantung, via Peking, by the fall of that year.

[137]Mao (A), 3 ts'e, pp. 95b-96b; Sun, Kuo-fu ch'üan-shu, p. 1052. Sun's eulogy for Chiang's deceased mother contains the following passages: "In ancient times Madame Liu of the T'ang dynasty encouraged her son, who later became a great scholar, to study by giving him pills made of bear's gall. Madame Ou-yang of the Sung dynasty taught her son, who also became a great scholar later on, to read by writing on the ground with a reed brush. I have only heard about such people but have never seen any like them. When I at last met Kai-shek, reflecting on his profound culture and godly breeding, I began to realize that even those people of ancient times were perhaps not to be compared with someone who is living in the present day." Adapted from Hsiung, pp. 137-38.

[138]Mao (A), 2 ts'e, p. 90a; 3 ts'e, p. 34a.

[139]Ibid., 3 ts'e, pp. 55b-56a.

[140]Ibid., pp. 67b-68b.

[141]Ibid., pp. 41a-b; 53a-b.

[142]Ibid., pp. 94b, 100b.

[143]Ibid., 4 ts'e, pp. 1a-2b, 8b-9b; Lo, Kuo-fu nien-p'u, vol. 2, pp. 809-10.

[144]Ibid., vol. 2, p. 812.

[145] Mao (A), 4 ts'e, p. 9b.

[146] Ibid., pp. 10a-13b.

[147] Ibid., pp. 15b-21a; Lo, Kuo-fu nien-p'u, vol. 2, pp. 816-20.

[148] Mao (A), 4 ts'e, pp. 21a-22b; Lo, Kuo-fu nien-p'u, vol. 2, pp. 820-30.

[149] Mao (A), 4 ts'e, p. 23a. For the various messages sent from May 1 to June 7 by Hsü Ch'ung-chih, Liao Chung-k'ai, Hu Han-min, Chang Chi, and Wang Ching-wei to request Chiang's return, see ibid., pp. 14, 16, 21b.

[150] Ibid., p. 24a-b.

[151] In February-March 1925 Chiang personally led the First Eastern Expedition against Ch'en Chiung-ming. He fought with a vengeance and won, at the cost of one-third of his 3,500-man army. See his preface to the First Whampoa Student Directory in ibid., 10 ts'e, p. 28b.

[152] Fu, p. 479.

[153] Mao (A), 4 ts'e, pp. 24a-27b. Sun's personal secretary Lin Chih-mien identified Chiang's official role on board the Yung-feng as chief-of-staff in the Field Headquarters; Lin Chih-mien and Chao Kuei-chang, "Sun ta-tsung-t'ung meng-nan chi kang-mu," in Chung-kuo Kuo-min-tang Kuang-tung sheng chih-hsing wei-yüan-hui, p. 61. Also see Feng Han-ming, "Sui-wei Sun ta-tsung-t'ung ch'u-shih chi," in Cheng Chao, p. 86.

[154] Sun was visited on board the Yung-feng by Wu T'ing-fang and Wei Pang-p'ing on June 17, by

Wang Ching-wei and Ku Ying-fen on July 3, and by
Chü Cheng and Ch'eng Ch'ien on August 8; but they
all returned ashore after the visits. Chiang
Chung-cheng, Sun ta-tsung-t'ung Kuang-chou meng-
nan jih-chi (Shanghai: Min chih shu-chü, June
1927), pp. 6, 19, 48. This booklet, originally
published in 1922, also appears in Chiang, Yen-lun
hui-pien, vol. 24, pp. 1-28.

Liao Chung-k'ai had been detained by Ch'en
Chiung-ming on June 14, two days before the coup.
Hu Han-min was in charge of the Generalissimo's
Headquarters at Shaokuan in the absence of Sun.
Also at the front taking part in the northern ex-
pedition were Hsü Ch'ung-chih, Li Lieh-chün, Chu
P'ei-te, Huang Ta-wei, and Li Fu-lin. Yang Shu-
k'an, Chang Chi, and many others were in Shanghai.
Chiang, Sun meng-nan jih-chi, p. 8; Lo, Kuo-fu
nien-p'u, vol. 2, pp. 823, 830-49; Hu Han-min,
"Tsung-li Kuang-chou meng-nan ching-kuo," in
Chung-kuo Kuo-min-tang Kuang-tung sheng chih-hsing
wei-yüan-hui, p. 31.

Among the lesser figures on board the Yung-
feng with Sun were secretaries Lin Chih-mien, Yang
Hsi-chi, Chou Chung-liang, and Ch'en Ch'ün; mili-
tary counselors Yang Hu, Hsieh Hsin-chun, and Lin
Shu-wei; aide-de-camp Ch'en Hsüan; bodyguards
Huang Hui-lung, Ma Hsiang, Li Yang-ching, and
Chiang Kuang-nai. Also present was Commander of
Maritime Defense Ch'en Ts'e. See Huang Hui-lung,
Chung-shan hsien-sheng ch'in-cheng, recorded by
Ch'en T'ieh-sheng (Shanghai: The Commercial Press,
August 1930), pp. 20, 26; photograph in Chung-kuo
Kuo-min-tang Kuang-tung sheng chih-hsing wei-yüan-
hui; Lin Chih-mien and Chao Kuei-chang; Feng Han-
ming, p. 86.

[155]Chiang, Sun meng-nan jih-chi, pp. 48-50;
Mao (A), 4 ts'e, pp. 27b-28a. It has been re-

ported that Sun made known his decision to leave
for Shanghai first to Commander of Maritime Defense Ch'en Ts'e and then to his secretary Lin Chih-
mien. This account seems to suggest that Chiang,
identified elsewhere as Sun's chief-of-staff, was
not consulted in advance. See Hu Wen-ts'an, "Sun
ta-tsung-t'ung Kuang-chou meng-nan shih li-chien
kuo-Hu chi-shu," in Chung-kuo Kuo-min-tang Kuang-
tung sheng chih-hsing wei-yüan-hui, p. 42.

[156]The date of publication of the first edition is given in the June 1927 edition of Chiang's
Sun meng-nan jih-chi, which I used. The manuscript
was completed on September 13, after Chiang's visit
with Chang Ching-chiang during his brief appearance
in Shanghai on September 9-11; Mao (A), 4 ts'e, p.
43a. For Sun's preface, dated October 10, see Sun,
Kuo-fu ch'üan-shu, p. 1054.

[157]The picture appears in many of the publications cited herein. See, for instance, Hsiung,
facing p. 78.

[158]Chiang Chung-cheng, "On the Centennial of
the Birth of Dr. Sun Yat-sen," Chung-yang jih-pao,
November 13, 1965, p. 1, for the English version;
and November 12, p. 1, for the Chinese version.

[159]Allen S. Whiting, Soviet Policies in China,
1917-1924 (New York: Columbia University Press,
1953), p. 184.

[160]Mao (A), 4 ts'e, p. 28b.

[161]Chiang Chung-cheng, "Yü Chang P'u-ch'üan
shu," August 27, 1922, in Tzu-fan lu, 1:4, 269.

[162]Mao (A), 4 ts'e, pp. 39a-40a; Sun, Kuo-fu
ch'üan-chi, p. 802. Sun had a conversation with

Joffe's representative on August 25; Lo, Kuo-fu nien-p'u, vol. 2, p. 852. Chiang's "diary" erroneously reports the event as "the first meeting between Mr. Sun and the Soviet representative Joffe"; Mao (A), 4 ts'e, p. 28b.

163 Ibid., pp. 29a-38a.

164 Ibid., pp. 38a-39a.

165 Ibid., p. 41a.

166 See Liao Chung-k'ai's letter of September 14 to Chiang, ibid., p. 42a-b.

167 Ibid., p. 41b; Sun, Kuo-fu ch'üan-chi, p. 804.

168 Mao (A), 4 ts'e, p. 41a.

169 Note 156 above.

170 Mao (A), 4 ts'e, pp. 47b-48a.

171 Ibid., p. 52a. For Chiang's suggestions for the military campaign in Fukien, sent to Hsü on the 8th, see ibid., pp. 48a-50a.

172 Ibid., p. 52b.

173 Ibid., pp. 54b-55a; adapted from Hsiung, p. 159.

174 Mao (A), 4 ts'e, p. 55b.

175 Ibid., pp. 56b-57a; Sun, Kuo-fu ch'üan-chi, p. 817; adapted from Hsiung, p. 160.

148

[176]Mao (A), 4 ts'e, pp. 56b, 60a, 66b; 5 ts'e, p. 2b. For Chiang's letter of December 11 to General Huang Ta-wei advising him to resign, see ibid., 4 ts'e, pp. 63b–66b.

[177]Ibid., 5 ts'e, p. 10b.

[178]Lo, Kuo-fu nien-p'u, vol. 2, pp. 877–78, 882–84, 889–90; George T. Yu, Party Politics in Republican China: The Kuomintang, 1912–1924 (Berkeley: University of California Press, 1966), pp. 168–71; Li Chien-nung, The Political History of China, 1840–1928, trans. and ed. by Ssu-yu Teng and Jeremy Ingalls (Princeton: D. Van Nostrand Co., 1956), pp. 442–43, 446–50. Sun had taken the initial step toward party reorganization on September 4, soon after his arrival in Shanghai following the Canton coup; Lo, Kuo-fu nien-p'u, vol. 2, pp. 853–54, 870. For the party manifesto and constitution, see Tsou Lu, vol. 1, pp. 345–52.

[179]Lo, Kuo-fu nien-p'u, vol. 2, pp. 890–93; Whiting, pp. 181–207; Li Yün-han, Ts'ung jung-Kung tao ch'ing-tang (Taipei: China Committee for Publication Aid and Prize Awards, 1966), vol. 1, pp. 139–50. For the Sun-Joffe Manifesto, see Tsou Lu, vol. 1, pp. 343–44; Leonard S. Hsü, Sun Yat-sen: His Political and Social Ideals (Los Angeles: University of Southern California Press, 1933), pp. 19–20.

[180]Mao (A), 5 ts'e, pp. 4b–9b; Chiang Chung-cheng, "Fu Liao Chung-k'ai shu," in Yen-lun hui-pien, vol. 24, pp. 90–92.

[181]Mao (A), 5 ts'e, p. 10b.

[182]Ibid., p. 10a–b.

[183] Ibid., p. 12b. A Central Cadres Confer-
ence of February 2, in which neither Sun nor Wang
took part, nominated a list of fifteen persons
that did not include Chiang. The final appointments, including Chiang, were made by Sun on the
3rd. See Lo, Kuo-fu nien-p'u, vol. 2, pp. 896-97.
Lo, citing party gazette, lists thirteen members;
Mao lists eleven.

[184] Mao (A), 5 ts'e, pp. 12b, 14b-16b.

[185] Tsou Lu, vol. 3, pp. 1065-75; Lo, Kuo-fu
nien-p'u, vol. 2, pp. 866-77, 880-81, 884-91,
893-94, 898-900; Mao (A), 4 ts'e, pp. 68b-69a; 5
ts'e, pp. 1b-4b, 16b-18a.

[186] Ibid., p. 17a-b.

[187] Ibid., pp. 19a-b, 23b-24a.

[188] Ibid., pp. 24b-25a.

[189] Ibid., pp. 20a-21b. The quotation is on
p. 21a.

[190] Ibid., pp. 21b-23b.

[191] Ibid., p. 24b.

[192] Ibid., pp. 26a-29b.

[193] Ibid., p. 29b; Lo, Kuo-fu nien-p'u, vol.
2, p. 910, citing gazette of the Generalissimo's
Headquarters.

[194] Mao (A), 5 ts'e, pp. 30a-40b; Lo, Kuo-fu
nien-p'u, vol. 2, pp. 915-35. For Chiang's dramatic role in the recapture of Shih-lung, see
Liang Lieh-ya, "Kuo-fu i-shih t'an," in Cheng

Chao, pp. 179–81. Facsimile of Sun's order appointing Chiang as chief-of-staff to the Generalissimo's Field Headquarters is dated June 16, not June 17 as in Mao; see "Ke-ming wen-hsien," in Li Hsü (no pagination).

[195] Chiang Chung-cheng, "Yü Yang Ts'ang-pai shu," July 13, 1923, in Yen-lun hui-pien, vol. 24, pp. 105-07. Chiang had wanted Liao to be in charge of finances, but Sun made him governor on May 7; Mao (A), 5 ts'e, p. 31a; Lo, Kuo-fu nien-p'u, vol. 2, p. 917.

[196] Mao (A), 5 ts'e, p. 4a-b. Chiang's reply is said to be missing.

During the month-long discussions between Liao Chung-k'ai and Joffe in February 1923 at the hot spring resort of Atami in Japan, they touched upon a number of areas of possible Kuomintang-Soviet cooperation, including a military training program. See C. Martin Wilbur and Julie Lien-ying How, eds., Documents on Communism, Nationalism, and Soviet Advisers in China, 1918-1927 (New York: Columbia University Press, 1956), p. 143, citing Fuse Katsuji, Su-O ti tung-fang cheng-ts'e (Soviet Russia's Policies in the East), trans. by Pan Su (5th ed., Shanghai: T'ai-p'ing-yang shu-tien, February 1929), pp. 229-32.

[197] No suggestion is intended that as of June-July 1923 a comprehensive plan existed for Soviet aid to the Kuomintang. It can be said with reasonable certainty, however, that Sun had by then decided to embark upon a new policy that involved an active search for Soviet political, financial, and military assistance.

A few historical notes on the emerging assistance program may be suggestive. On October 6,

151

1923 Borodin arrived in Canton. See Wilbur and
How, p. 144; Lo, Kuo-fu nien-p'u, vol. 2, p. 956;
Robert C. North, Moscow and Chinese Communists
(2nd ed., Stanford: Stanford University Press,
1963), p. 74; Chiang Yung-ching, Pao-lo-t'ing yü
Wu-Han cheng-ch'üan (Taipei: China Committee for
Publication Aid and Prize Awards, December 1963),
p. 5. With him came two military officers; two
others joined him in January 1924. In June a General Pavlov arrived in Canton, followed during the
next month by six Soviet military men "and others." See A.I. Cherepanov, Zapiski Voennogo
Sovetnika v Kitai; iz Istorii Perovi Grazhdanskoi
Revolutsionnoi Voiny, 1924-1927 (Moscow: Academy
of Sciences of the USSR), vol. 1, pp. 31 and 107;
I am indebted to Professor C. Martin Wilbur for
this reference. The first shipment of Soviet war
matériel, consisting of 8,000 rifles with 500
rounds of ammunition for each, did not reach
Whampoa until October 7, fully a year after the
arrival of Borodin. See F.F. Liu, A Military History of Modern China, 1924-1949 (Princeton: Princeton University Press, 1956), p. 14; Mao (A), 8
ts'e, p. 2b. According to one source, "the total
cost of supplies shipped on credit to Canton up to
December 1 [1925] amounted to 2,000,000 roubles";
Wilbur and How, p. 169. Another work notes that
"Russian aid was not . . . as generous as it was
reported to be. Its quantity was meager, its
quality low." See Liu, p. 27. During 1924 the
Soviet Union also extended a grant of three mil-
lion roubles for the "organization and early run-
ning expenses" of the Whampoa Academy; Louis
Fischer, The Soviets in World Affairs: A History
of the Relations Between the Soviet Union and the
Rest of the World, 1917-1929 (2nd ed., Princeton:
Princeton University Press, 1951), vol. 2, p. 640.
Also see Roderick L. MacFarquhar, "The Whampoa

152

Military Academy," Papers on China, vol. 10, 1955, pp. 146-72.

[198] Chiang Kai-shek, Soviet Russia in China: A Summing-Up at Seventy (New York: Farrar, Straus & Cudahy, 1957), p. 19; Mao (A), 5 ts'e, p. 41a.

[199] Ibid., pp. 41b, 44b, 48a. For further information on Chiang's trip until his return to Shanghai on December 15, see ibid., pp. 41b-74a, passim; Chiang, Soviet Russia in China, pp. 19-24.

[200] Whiting, p. 243, citing typed copy from the original file of Sun-Karakhan correspondence in the personal collection of Louis Fischer.

[201] Chiang Chung-cheng, "Fu shang tsung-li shu," March 2, 1924, in Yen-lun hui-pien, vol. 24, p. 74. On August 19, 1923 Chiang wrote from Dairen that he would be gone for a long time but did not specify how long: "From here on the journey will grow increasingly distant. I do not know when I shall be able to return home to sweep [my mother's] grave." Chiang Chung-cheng, "K'an ai-ssu-lu so kan," in Mao (A), 5 ts'e, p. 43a, and in Yen-lun hui-pien, vol. 24, p. 67.

For Sun's eastern expedition, see Ku Ying-fen, Min-kuo shih-erh nien Sun ta-yüan-shuai tung-cheng jih-chi (Shanghai: Min-chih shu-chü, November 1926); Lo, Kuo-fu nien-p'u, vol. 2, pp. 939-77.

[202] Mao (A), 5 ts'e, pp. 73b-74a.

[203] Ibid., pp. 77b-78a.

[204] Ibid., p. 78a-b. Chiang's letters are not given in Mao and cannot be located elsewhere, but his views are reflected in the letters he received.

[205] Ibid., 6 ts'e, p. 1a.

[206] Chiang Chung-cheng, "Pen-tang tsui-chin chung-yao wen-t'i," in Tzu-fan lu, 2:15, 1501; George E. Sokolsky, "The Kuomintang," China Year Book, 1929-30, p. 1200. For the roster of delegates to the First National Congress, see Lo, Ke-ming wen-hsien, vol. 8, pp. 1100-03. In 1956 Chiang criticized the actions of the Chinese Communists and certain Kuomintang members at the Congress, but without saying that he himself had attended the Congress. See Chiang, Soviet Russia in China, p. 25.

[207] Yang Shu-k'an was appointed to succeed Liao Chung-k'ai. See Lo, Kuo-fu nien-p'u, vol. 2, p. 1003, citing gazette of the Generalissimo's Headquarters.

[208] Mao (A), 6 ts'e, pp. 2a-3a, 6a-7a; Lo, Kuo-fu nien-p'u, vol. 2, pp. 1003, 1010-13.

[209] Liu, p. 9; Chiang, Soviet Russia in China, p. 25.

[210] Chiang, "Fu shang tsung-li shu," pp. 74-79; Mao (A), 6 ts'e, pp. 8b-20b. Yang Shu-k'an submitted his resignation on June 2; ibid., 7 ts'e, p. 1a. He was replaced by Liao on June 12; see Lo, Kuo-fu nien-p'u, vol. 2, p. 1029.

[211] Chiang Chung-cheng, "Fu Liao Chung-k'ai shu," March 14, 1924, in Yen-lun hui-pien, vol. 24, pp. 93-97; Mao (A), 6 ts'e, pp. 20b-31a.

[212] Ibid., pp. 34b-39a.

[213] Ibid., pp. 41b-43b; Chiang, Yen-lun hui-pien, vol. 24, p. 110.

[214]Mao (A), 6 ts'e, p. 44b. In his military report to the Second National Congress of the Kuomintang on January 6, 1926, Chiang said the financial administration of Kwangtung in mid-1924 was "completely" controlled by the Yunnan and Kwangsi armies of Yang Hsi-min and Liu Chen-huan. Ibid., 14 ts'e, p. 7a.

[215]Ibid., 6 ts'e, p. 45a.

[216]See communications from Hu Han-min, Liao Chung-k'ai, Wang Ching-wei, and Tai Chi-t'ao, in ibid., 5 ts'e, pp. 77a-78b; 6 ts'e, pp. 31a-34a, 39b-40a, 46b.

[217]Ibid., p. 47a-b.

[218]Ibid., p. 53b; Lo, Kuo-fu nien-p'u, vol. 2, pp. 1022, 1024, 1034, citing Kuomintang Archives.

[219]Liu, p. 10.

[220]Chiang was never officially a generalissimo. Until his election in 1948 as president under the new constitution, he was better known as chairman, referring to his chairmanship of the Military Council.

[221]Mao (A), 7 ts'e, pp. 43a-66a; 8 ts'e, pp. 5b-26b, passim; Sun, Kuo-fu ch'üan-chi, pp. 842-43; "Tsung-li chi Chung-kuo Kuo-min-tang kuan-yü ch'u-li shang-t'uan shih-pien chih wen-chien," in Lo, Ke-ming wen-hsien, vol. 10, pp. 1473-83; Lo, Kuo-fu nien-p'u, vol. 2, pp. 1047-57, 1072-75; Wilbur and How, pp. 155-56.

[222]Mao (A), 7 ts'e, p. 62b. For Chiang's remark, see his military report to the Second

National Congress of the Kuomintang, January 6, 1926, _ibid._, 14 ts'e, pp. 8b-9a.

223_Ibid._, 8 ts'e, pp. 6b-8b; Sun, Kuo-fu ch'üan-chi, p. 845. The Revolutionary Committee was formally inaugurated on October 11, with Sun as chairman. Wang Ching-wei was one of the seven members, the others being Chiang Kai-shek, Hsü Ch'ung-chih, Liao Chung-k'ai, Ch'en Yu-jen (Eugene Ch'en), and T'an P'ing-shan. On October 14 Hu Han-min was named acting chairman of the Committee. Chiang's demands were thus completely met. Lo, Kuo-fu nien-p'u, vol. 2, p. 1074; Mao (A), 8 ts'e, pp. 15b-16a.

224_Ibid._, pp. 3a-5b.

225_Ibid._, 7 ts'e, pp. 57b-60a; 8 ts'e, pp. 2a-37a, passim; Sun, Kuo-fu ch'üan-chi, pp. 843-44; Lo, Kuo-fu nien-p'u, vol. 2, pp. 1059-60, 1065-66, 1071, citing gazette of the Generalissimo's Headquarters, no. 27; Wilbur and How, pp. 154-55.

226Mao (A), 7 ts'e, pp. 26a-27a; 8 ts'e, pp. 6b, 22b-23a; Lo, Kuo-fu nien-p'u, vol. 2, pp. 1038, 1039-40, 1057, 1086. Lo identifies Chiang as chairman of the Military Council as of October 14 (ibid., p. 1074); this is, however, not corroborated by the "diary" nor supported by other documentary sources.

227It is interesting to note that Chiang did not receive news of Sun's death on March 12 from Acting Generalissimo Hu Han-min until the 21st. See Chiang, Tzu-fan lu, 1:2, 163-64. This information appears incorrectly in the "diary" under the March 27 entry; see Mao (A), 9 ts'e, pp. 79a-80a.

156

[228] For Chiang's rise to power after Sun's death, see Pichon P.Y. Loh, "The Politics of Chiang Kai-shek: A Reappraisal," *Journal of Asian Studies*, vol. 25, no. 3 (May 1966), pp. 433-43. For an inquiry into Chiang's personality and politics during the Sian coup of December 1936, see Pichon P.Y. Loh, "The Politics of Chiang Kai-shek: His Policy of Unity," a paper presented before the Columbia University Seminar on Modern East Asia: China, February 21, 1968, pp. 9-14, 30-31.

[229] Lo, *Kuo-fu nien-p'u*, vol. 2, pp. 1086-88.

[230] Cf. Schiffrin; Lyon Sharman, *Sun Yat-sen, His Life and Its Meaning: A Critical Biography* (Hamden: Archon Books, [1934] 1965).

[231] Mao (A), 8 ts'e, pp. 49b-50a. This passage has been translated by Chiang as follows: "Having seen the spirit of this Academy, I know it can carry on my revolutionary task. Even if I should die, my conscience will be at peace." See Chiang, *Soviet Russia in China*, p. 35.

[232] Mao (A), 9 ts'e, p. 78a (emphasis added). For another account of the same conversation, see Chiang Chung-cheng, "Tsung-li tui chün-hsiao tsui shen-ch'ieh ti chiao-hsün," April 5, 1925, in *Yen-lun hui-pien*, vol. 8, p. 176; and Mao (A), 19 ts'e, pp. 3b-4a.

[233] Chiang Chung-cheng, "Hui-fu ke-ming ching-shen ho chi-lü," February 11, 1928, in *Yen-lun hui-pien*, vol. 9, p. 53. Also see Chiang Chung-cheng, "Chi tsung-li wen," March 30, 1925, *ibid.*, vol. 24, pp. 131-32; and Mao (A), 9 ts'e, pp. 84b-86b.

234For a discussion of Chiang's ideological indebtedness to Sun, see Pichon P.Y. Loh, "The Ideological Persuasion of Chiang Kai-shek," Modern Asian Studies, vol. 4, part 3 (July 1970), pp. 211-38.

235Karen Horney, who modified Freud's "scientific" psychoanalysis by introducing "moral" issues of "judgments as to right and wrong" in a psychocultural context, presents us with three non-exclusive neurotic personality types. These three types—not a study in typology but a "simplification for persons with distinct characteristics," a classificatory schema for therapeutic convenience—are the compliant, the aggressive, and the detached. Their predominant attitudes are, respectively, "moving toward people," "moving against people," and "moving away from people." Since Horney's types stress attitudinal predispositions and interpersonal dynamics as well as societal norms, they are instructive for persons interested in the social sciences and in political psychology. Karen Horney, Our Inner Conflicts: A Constructive Theory of Neurosis (New York: W.W. Norton & Co., 1945, 1966), pp. 40-47, 48-49 note 1, 177.

Allowing for cultural differences, Horney's description of the aggressive type with the predominant attitude of moving against people seems to describe exceedingly well Chiang's personality. The reader may be as interested as the present writer in the following quotations:

> While the compliant type tends to appease, the aggressive type does everything he can to be a good fighter. He is alert and keen in an argument and will go out of his way to launch one for the sake of proving he is right. He may be at his best when his back

is to the wall and there is no alternative
but to fight. In contrast to the compliant type who is afraid to win a game, he
is a bad loser and undeniably wants victory.
He is just as ready to accuse others as the
former is to take blame on himself. In neither case does the consideration of guilt
play a role. The compliant type when he
pleads guilty is by no means convinced that
he is so, but is driven to appease. The
aggressive type similarly is not convinced
that the other fellow is wrong; he just as-
sumes he is right because he needs this
ground of subjective certainty in much the
same way as an army needs a safe point
from which to launch an attack. To admit
an error when it is not absolutely necessary seems to him an unforgivable display
of weakness, if not errant foolishness.

It is consistent with his attitude of
having to fight against a malevolent world
that he should develop a keen sense of
realism--of its kind. He will never be so
"naïve" as to overlook in others any mani-
festation of ambition, greed, ignorance,
or anything else that might obstruct his
own goals. Since in a competitive civili-
zation attributes like these are much more
common than real decency, he feels justified in regarding himself as only realistic. Actually, of course, he is just as
one-sided as the compliant type. Another
facet of his realism is his emphasis on
planning and foresight. Like any good
strategist, in every situation he is
careful to appraise his own chances, the
forces of his adversaries, and the possible pitfalls.

159

Because he is driven always to assert
himself as the strongest, shrewdest, or
most sought after, he tries to develop the
efficiency and resourcefulness necessary
to being so. The zest and intelligence he
puts into his work may make him a highly
esteemed employee or a success in a business of his own. However, the impression
he gives of having an absorbing interest in
his work will in a sense be misleading, because for him work is only a means to an
end. He has no love for what he is doing
and takes no real pleasure in it--a fact
consistent with his attempt to exclude
feelings from his life altogether. This
choking off of all feeling has a two-
edged effect. On the one hand it is undoubtedly expedient from the standpoint of
success in that it enables him to function
like a well-oiled machine, untiringly pro-
ducing the goods that will bring him ever
more power and prestige. . . . On the other
hand the emotional barrenness that results
from a throttling of feeling will do something to the quality of his work; certainly
it is bound to detract from his creativity.
. . . His feeling about himself is that
he is strong, honest, and realistic, all of
which is true if you look at things his way.
According to his premises his estimate of
himself is strictly logical, since to him
ruthlessness is strength, lack of consideration for others, honesty, and a callous
pursuit of one's own ends, realism. His
attitude on the score of his honesty comes
partly from a shrewd debunking of current
hypocrisies. Enthusiasm for a case, phil-
anthropic sentiments, and the like he sees
as sheer pretense, and it is not hard for

160

him to expose gestures of social consciousness or Christian virtue for what they so often are. His set of values is built around the philosophy of the jungle. Might makes right. Away with humaneness and mercy. <u>Homo homini lupus</u>. Here we have values not very different from those with which the nazis have made us so familiar.

There is subjective logic in the tendency of the aggressive type to reject real sympathy and friendliness as well as their counterfeits, compliance and appeasement. But it would be a mistake to assume that he cannot tell the difference. When he meets with an indubitably friendly spirit coupled with strength he is well able to recognize and respect it. The point is that he believes it to be against his interest to be too discriminating in this respect. Both attitudes strike him as liabilities in the battle for survival.

Why, though, does he reject the softer human sentiments with such violence . . . ? He acts like the man who chased beggars from his door because they were breaking his heart. . . . Actually, his feelings on the score of "softness" in others are mixed. He despises it in them, it is true, but he welcomes it as well, because it leaves him all the freer to pursue his own goals. Why else should he so often feel drawn toward the compliant type--just as the latter is often drawn toward him? The reason his reaction is so extreme is that it is prompted by his need to fight all softer feelings within himself. . . . In the case of the beggar, for instance, he would have stirrings of real sympathy, a need to comply with the request, a feeling that he ought to be helpful. But there is a

still greater need to push all this away
from him.

The hope of fusing his divergent drives,
which the compliant type places in love, is
sought by the aggressive in recognition.
To be recognized promises him not only the
affirmation of himself he requires but holds
out the additional lure of being liked by
others and of being able in turn to like
them. Since recognition thus appears to offer solution of his conflicts, it becomes the
saving mirage he pursues.

Ibid., pp. 66-70. If moving against people was
the predominant attitude in Chiang, moving away
from people was an attitude second in prominence.
Horney describes the detached type in the following terms:

What is crucial is their inner need to put
emotional distance between themselves and
others. More accurately, it is their conscious determination not to get emotionally
involved with others in any way, whether in
love, fight, co-operation, or competition.
They draw around themselves a kind of magic
circle which no one may penetrate. And this
is why, superficially, they may "get along"
with people. The compulsive character of the
need shows up in their reaction of anxiety
when the world intrudes on them.
All the needs and qualities they acquire
are directed toward this major need of not
getting involved. Among the most striking
is a need for self-sufficiency. . . .
Another pronounced need is his need for
privacy. . . .
Self-sufficiency and privacy both serve
his most outstanding need, the need for utter independence. . . .

162

The need to feel superior, although common to all neuroses, must be stressed here
because of its intrinsic association with
detachment. . . . Probably nobody can stand
isolation without either being particularly
strong and resourceful or feeling uniquely
significant.

Ibid., pp. 75-79.

Horney thus brings to our attention the two
psychological processes by which the neurotic at-
tempts to dispose of his inner conflicts. One is
to repress certain aspects of his conflicts and to
build a personality structure on their opposites.
The other is to hold oneself aloof from people so
that the basic neurotic conflicts have no chance
to manifest themselves. Common to both processes
is the creation of an idealized image, which the
neurotic "believes himself to be" or which he
"feels he can or ought to be." Horney describes
the relatively unified idealized image of neurotic
Z as follows:

In the factual behavior of Z aggressive
trends strongly predominated, accompanied by
sadistic tendencies. He was domineering and
inclined to exploit. Driven by a devouring
ambition, he pushed ruthlessly ahead. He
could plan, organize, fight, and adhered con-
sciously to an unmitigated jungle philosophy.
He was also extremely detached; but since his
aggressive drives always entangled him with
groups of people, he could not maintain his
aloofness. He kept strict guard, though, not
to get involved in any personal relationship
nor to let himself enjoy anything to which
people were essential contributors. In this
he succeeded fairly well, because positive
feelings for others were greatly repressed;
desires for human intimacy were mainly chan-

163

neled along sexual lines. There was present,
however, a distinct tendency to comply, together with a need for approval that inter-
fered with his craving for power. And there
were underlying puritanical standards, used
chiefly as a whip over others--but which of
course he could not help applying to himself
as well--that clashed headlong with his jungle philosophy.

In his idealized image he was the knight
in shining armor, the crusader with wide and
unfailing vision, ever pursuing the right.
As becomes a wise leader, he was not personally attached to anyone but dispensed a stern
though just discipline. He was honest without being hypocritical. Women loved him and
he could be a great lover but was not tied to
any woman. . . .

The idealized image is thus an attempt at
solving the basic conflict. . . . It has the
enormous subjective value of serving as a
binder, of holding together a divided individual. And although it exists only in the
person's mind, it exerts a decisive influence on his relations with others.

From this and other examples, Horney general-
ized concerning the idealized image:

The idealized image might be called a fictitious or illusory self, but that would be
only a half truth and hence misleading. The
wishful thinking operating in its creation is
certainly striking, particularly since it occurs in persons who otherwise stand on a
ground of firm reality. But this does not
make it wholly fictitious. It is an imagina-
tive creation interwoven with and determined
by very realistic factors. It usually contains traces of the person's genuine ideals.

164

While the grandiose achievements are illusory, the potentialities underlying them are
often real. More relevant, it is born of
very real inner necessities, it fulfills
very real functions, and it has a very real
influence on its creator. . . . Looking back
over the history of many patients we are led
to believe that its establishment has often
been literally lifesaving, and that is why
the resistance a patient puts up if his image is attacked is entirely justified, or at
least logical. As long as his image remains
real to him and is intact, he can feel significant, superior, and harmonious, in spite
of the illusory nature of those feelings. He
can consider himself entitled to raise all
kinds of demands and claims on the basis of
his assumed superiority. But if he allows it
to be undermined he is immediately threatened
with the prospect of facing all his weaknesses, with no title to special claims, a com-
paratively insignificant figure or even--in
his own eyes--a contemptible one.

Ibid., pp. 107-09 (emphasis added).

[236]Erik Erikson views the individual as a
creative agent enjoying considerable freedom in
the construction and development of his personality. He postulates "eight ages of man," culminat-
ing in the age of "maturity" in which the principal inner conflict is characterized as the "integrity crisis" or the struggle between "ego integrity" and "despair." He presents the notion of "ego
integrity" in the following terms:

Only in him who in some way has taken care
of things and people and has adapted himself
to the triumphs and disappointments adherent
to being, the originator of others or the

generator of products and ideas--only in him
may gradually ripen the fruit of these seven
stages [that precede the integrity crisis].
I know no better word for it than ego integrity. Lacking a clear definition, I shall
point to a few constituents of this state of
mind. It is the ego's accrued assurance of
its proclivity for order and meaning. It is
a post-narcissistic love of the human ego--
not of the self--as an experience which con-
veys some world order and spiritual sense,
no matter how dearly paid for. It is the ac-
ceptance of one's one and only life cycle as
something that had to be and that, by necessity, permitted of no substitutions: it thus
means a new, a different love of one's parents. It is a comradeship with the ordering
ways of distant time and different pursuits,
as expressed in the simple products and say-
ings of such times and pursuits. Although
aware of the relativity of all the various
life styles which have given meaning to human striving, the possessor of integrity is
ready to defend the dignity of his own life
style against all physical and economic
threats. For he knows that an individual
life is the accidental coincidence of but
one life cycle with but one segment of history; and that for him all human integrity
stands or falls with the one style of integrity of which he partakes. The style of integrity developed by his culture or civiliza-
tion thus becomes the "patrimony of his
soul," the seal of his moral paternity of
himself. . . . In such final consolation,
death loses its sting.

See Erikson, Childhood and Society, p. 268.

166

While it may be argued that Chiang lacked
some of the preconditions for ego integrity--such
as the development of "basic trust" over "mistrust," said to be characteristic of the very
first, oral-sensory, stage of the life cycle--it
may be said that Chiang, within the limits of his
psychological capability, compensated for his lack
by constructing an idealized self-image and
through other conscious and subconscious devices.
That the psychological mechanisms he resorted to
produced certain "undesirable" social and clinical
personality traits I will not argue. What I wish
to stress is that Chiang made a strenuous effort
to regain his psychological balance, acted as a
creative agent in the development of his personality, decided upon a life career and a life style,
and emerged from the delayed identity crisis and
precocious integrity crisis during the early twenties with "a few constituents" Erikson identifies
with the notion of ego integrity. Having done
this, Chiang stood ready "to defend the dignity of
his own life style against all physical and economic threats" and rested assured that "all human
integrity stands or falls with the one style of
integrity of which he partakes."

Erikson sees the telescoped nature of life
crises as more common to the religionists. Where
this life experience occurs, it creates for the
religionist the "problem of existential identity."
Concerning this, he offers the following analysis:

This integrity crisis, last in the lives
of ordinary men, is a life-long and chronic
crisis in a homo religiosus. . . .
This short cut between the youthful crisis of identity and the mature one of integrity makes the religionist's problem of individual identity the same as the problem of
existential identity. To some extent this

problem is only an exaggeration of an abortive trait not uncommon in late adolescence. One may say that the religious leader becomes a professional in dealing with the kind of scruples which prove transitory in many all-too-serious postadolescents who later grow out of it, go to pieces over it, or find an intellectual or artistic medium which can stand between them and nothingness.

The late adolescent crisis, in addition to anticipating the more mature crises, can at the same time hark back to the very earliest crisis of life--trust or mistrust toward existence as such. This concentration in the cataclysm of the adolescent identity crisis of both first and last crises in the human life may well explain why religiously and artistically creative men often seem to be suffering from a barely compensated psychosis, and yet later prove superhumanly gifted in conveying a total meaning for man's life; while malignant disturbances in late adolescence often display precocious wisdom and usurped integrity. The chosen young man extends the problem of his identity to the borders of existence in the known universe; other human beings bend all their efforts to adopt and fulfill the departmentalized identities which they find prepared in their communities. He can permit himself to face as permanent the trust problem which drives others in whom it remains or becomes dominant into denial, despair, and psychosis. He acts as if mankind were starting all over with his own beginning as an individual, conscious of his singularity as well as his humanity; others hide in the folds of whatever tradition they are part of because of membership, occupation, or special interests. To him, history

168

ends as well as starts with him; others must
look to their memories, to legends, or to
books to find models for the present and the
future in what their predecessors have said
and done.

Erikson, Young Man Luther, pp. 261-62.

Erikson gives two examples of abortive premature integrity crisis as it relates to the political man. He mentions Hamlet: "Shakespeare's
Hamlet, a very late adolescent with a premature,
royal integrity, and still deeply involved with
his oedipal conflicts, poses the question 'to be
or not to be' as a sublime choice." Ibid., p.
113. He also cites the young Hitler as having experienced something of a precocious integrity crisis at the age of fifteen, when he felt a compulsion to rebuild the world that was then his, his
hometown Linz, Austria. Erikson comments: "This
account illustrates the eerie balance between de-
structiveness and constructiveness, between sui-
cidal Nothingness and dictatorial Allness, in a
young man who at fifteen 'felt responsible for
everything that was being built,' that is, was
dominated by an overweening conscience and a kind
of premature integrity such as characterizes all
ideological leaders; he had selected, with deadly
obsessiveness, his medium of salvation: architec-
ture." Ibid., pp. 107-08.

The basic unresolved theoretical question,
given the Eriksonian life cycle, is whether or not
precocious integrity crisis is at all compatible
with political leadership and the societal function
of "authoritative allocation of values."

237Rufus P. Browning, "The Interaction of Personality and Political System in Decisions to Run
for Office: Some Data and a Simulation Technique,"
Journal of Social Issues, vol. 24, no. 3 (July

1968), pp. 93-109. Browning observes that "high levels of achievement and power motivation and low levels of affiliative concern appear in these data as a distinctive syndrome closely related to vigorous influencing and efforts to achieve success in whatever arena" (p. 98).

[238]Cf. Herbert McClosky, "Conservatism and Personality," American Political Science Review, vol. 52, no. 1 (March 1958), pp. 27-45.

[239]For a review of the stratification, structural-functional, self-selection (personality), and political socialization hypotheses of leadership recruitment, see Kenneth Prewitt, "Political Socialization and Leadership Selection," The Annals of the American Academy of Political and Social Science, vol. 361, September 1965, pp. 96-111.

GLOSSARY

Anfu Clique	安福系
Atami	熱海
Boca Tigris	虎門礮台
Bureau of Rice Control	平糴局
Central Cadres Conference	中央幹部會議
Chang Chi	張繼
Chang Chih-tung	張之洞
Chang Ching-chiang	張靜江
Chang Ch'ün	張羣
Chang T'ai-lei	張太雷
Chang Tso-lin	張作霖
Ch'angchow Fortress	長州要塞
Chao-ho incident	肇和事件
Ch'en Chi-t'ang	陳濟棠
Ch'en Ch'i-mei	陳其美
Ch'en Chiung-ming	陳炯明
Ch'en Ch'un-hsüan	岑春煊
Ch'en Ch'ün	陳羣
Ch'en Hsüan	陳煊
Ch'en K'o-yü	陳可鈺
Ch'en Kuo-fu	陳果夫
Ch'en Pu-lei	陳布雷
Ch'en Shao-pai	陳少白

171

Ch'en Shun 陳順

Ch'en Ts'e 陳策

Ch'en Yu-jen 陳友仁

Cheng hsien 嵊縣

Ch'eng Ch'ien 程潛

Ch'eng T'ien-fang 程天放

Chengtu 成都

Ch'i-k'ou 溪口

Chiang Chieh-shih (Kai-shek) 蔣介石
  Chung-cheng 中正
  Jui-yüan 瑞元

Chiang Chin-fan 蔣謹藩

Chiang Ching-kuo 蔣經國

Chiang Jui-ch'ing 蔣瑞青

Chiang Jui-chü 蔣瑞菊

Chiang Jui-ch'un 蔣瑞春

Chiang Jui-lien 蔣瑞蓮

Chiang Hsi-hou 蔣錫侯

Chiang Monlin 蔣夢麟

Chiang Su-an 蔣肅菴

Chiang Wei-kuo 蔣緯國

Chiang Yü-piao 蔣玉表

chiao-tzu yu-fang 教子有方

Chien-chin hsüeh-t'ang 箭金學堂

ch'ien-chün i-fa 千鈞一髮

Chihli Clique 直隸系

ching, ching, tan, i 靜敬澹一

172

Chinwangtao	秦皇島
Chou Chung-liang	周仲良
Chou Jih-hsüan	周日宣
Chou li	周禮
Chü Cheng	居正
Chu Chih-hsin Ta-fu	朱執信 大符
Chu Ching-sung	竺景崧
Chu, Mr.	朱君
Chu P'ei-te	朱培德
chu shih	竹詩
chüan	卷
Ch'üan-hsüeh p'ien	勸學篇
Chuang-tzu	莊子
Ch'un Ch'iu	春秋
Chün-sheng tsa-chih	軍聲雜誌
Chung-hua ke-ming-tang	中華革命黨
S.S. Chung-kuo	中國號
Chung-yung	中庸
Fan Shih-sheng	范石生
Fang-hai chi-lüeh	防海紀略
Feng-lu hsüeh-t'ang	鳳麓學堂
Feng Yü-hsiang	馮玉祥
Feng-hua	奉化
Fengtien Clique	奉天系
Ho Ts'ui-lien	何淬廉 （何廉）
Hsiang-tao chou-pao	嚮導週報

173

<u>Hsiao ching</u>	孝經
hsiao-nao tso-yung	小腦作用
Hsiao-sha-tu (Siau Soo Doo)	小沙渡
Hsieh Ch'ih	謝持
Hsieh Hsin-chun	謝心準
<u>Hsin-ch'ao</u>	新潮
<u>Hsin ch'ing-nien</u>	新青年
Hsiung, S.I.	熊式一
Hsü Ch'ung-chih	許崇智
Hu Han-min	胡漢民
Hu I-sheng	胡毅生
Hu Lin-i	胡林翼
<u>Hu Wen-chung kung i-chi</u>	胡文忠公遺集
Huang Chi-lu	黃季陸
Huang Fu	黃郛
Huang Hui-lung	黃惠龍
Huang Ta-wei	黃大偉
i-chih pan-chieh	一知半解
<u>I ching</u>	易經
Jen Chieh-mei	仕介眉
<u>Ju-lin wai-shih</u>	儒林外史
<u>Ke-ming chün</u>	革命軍
Kiangnan Arsenal	江南製造局
Kiangyin Fortress	江陰礮台
Ko-ch'i	葛溪
Ku Ch'ing-lien	顧清廉

174

Ku Ying-fen	古應芬
Kuang-fu-hui	光復會
Kuomintang	國民黨
Kweilin	桂林
li	禮
Li chi	禮記
Li Chi-shen	李濟深
Li Fu-lin	李富林
Li Lieh-chün	李烈鈞
Li-tai t'ung-chien chi-lan	歷代通鑑輯覽
Li Tsung-jen	李宗仁
Li Yang-ching	李揚敬
Liang-shan	梁山
Liao Chung-k'ai	廖仲愷
Lin Chen-hsiung	林振雄
Lin Chih-mien	林直勉
Lin Sen	林森
Lin Shu-wei	林樹巍
Lin Tsu-han	林祖涵
Lin Yeh-ming	林業明
Liu Chen-huan	劉震寰
Liu, Madame	柳（仲郢之母）
Lo Chia-lun	羅家倫
Loyang	洛陽
Lu Chiu-yüan	陸九淵
Lü Ch'un-jung	呂春榮

175

Lu Hsiang-shan ch'üan-chi	陸象山全集
Lu Yung-hsiang	盧永祥
Lun yü	論語
Lung-ching chung-hsüeh-t'ang	龍津中學堂
Ma Hsiang	馬湘
Mao Feng-mei	毛鳳美
Mao, Miss	毛氏
Mao Ssu-ch'eng	毛思誠
Meng-tzu	孟子
Merchant Corps	商團
Ming chien	明鑑
nai-ho	奈何
Nanning	南寧
Ningpo	寧波
Ou-yang, Madame	歐陽 (修之母)
P'eng Hsüeh-ch'in	彭學琴
P'ing Che chi-lüeh	平浙紀略
Preparatory Committee for the Military Training of All Armies	各軍軍事訓練籌備委員會
Revolutionary Committee	革命委員會
Shao Yüan-ch'ung	邵元沖
Shaokuan	韶關
Shen Hung-ying	沈鴻英
Shen Ting-i	沈定一
Shenyang	瀋陽

shih-chieh kung-ho ta-kuo	世界共和大國
Shih ching	詩經
Shih-lung	石龍
Shimbu Gakkō	振武學校
Shu ching	書經
Shui-hu chuan	水滸傳
Shuo wen	說文
Soochow	蘇州
Sun Hung-i	孫洪伊
Sun K'o	孫科
Sun-tzu ping-fa	孫子兵法
Sun Chung-shan (Yat-sen)	孫中山（逸仙）
Sung chien	宋鑑
Swatow	汕頭
Ta-hsüeh	大學
Tai Chi-t'ao	戴季陶
Taiping	太平
T'ai-p'ing t'ien-kuo wai-lüeh	太平天國外略
Takada	高田
T'an P'ing-shan	譚平山
T'an Yen-k'ai	譚延闓
T'ang Leang-li	湯良禮
T'ang Shao-i	唐紹儀
T'ao Ch'eng-chang	陶成章
Teng K'eng	鄧鏗
Teng Tse-ju	鄧澤如

177

Teng Yen-ta	鄧演達
Tientsin	天津
Ting Ching-liang	丁景梁
Ting-i ts'ung-k'an	定夷叢刊
Tong, Hollington K.	董顯光
Training Board of the Kwangtung Army Headquarters	粵軍總司令部 訓練部
Tseng Kuo-fan	曾國藩
Tseng Wen-cheng kung chia shu	曾文正公家書
Tseng Wen-cheng kung ch'üan-chi	曾文正公全集
Tseng Yüan-fu	曾沅甫
Tso chuan	左傳
Tso Tsung-t'ang	左宗棠
Tsou Lu	鄒魯
Tsou Jung	鄒容
Ts'ung-hsün chai-yü	聰訓齋語
Tuan Ch'i-jui	段祺瑞
T'ung-chien kang-mu	通鑑綱目
Tung-fang tsa-chih	東方雜誌
T'ung-kuo lu-chün su-ch'eng hsüeh-t'ang	通國陸軍速成學堂
T'ung-meng-hui	同盟會
tu-tu (tutuh)	都督
Wang Ching-wei	汪精衛
Wang Po-ling	王伯齡
Wang Teng-yün	王登雲
Wang Ts'ai-yü	王采玉

Wang Yang-ming	王陽明
Wei Pang-p'ing	魏邦平
Western Hill	西山
Whampoa Military Academy	黄埔陸軍軍官學校
Wu Chung-hsin	吳忠信
Wu P'ei-fu	吳佩孚
Wu T'ing-fang	吳廷芳
Wuhsi	無錫
Wu-ling	武嶺
Yang Hu	楊虎
Yang Hsi-chi	楊熙績
Yang Hsi-min	楊希閔
Yang Hsi-yen	楊西巖
Yang Shu-k'an	楊庶湛
Yao, Miss	姚氏
Yao Tsung-yüan	姚宗元
Yen Hsi-shan	閻錫山
Yen-t'ai Naval Academy	煙台海軍學校
Yo Fei	岳飛
Yü Chien-kuang	余建光
Yü Fei-p'eng	俞飛鵬
Yü Yu-jen	于右任
Yüan chien	元鑑
Yüan Shih-k'ai	袁世凱
Yutai (Yü-t'ai) Salt Store	玉泰鹽舖
Yung-feng, S.S.	永豐艦

BIBLIOGRAPHY

Adorno, T.W., Else Frenkel-Brunswik, Daniel J.
    Levinson, and R. Nevitt Sanford. The Authori-
    tarian Personality. New York: Harper & Row,
    1950.
Almond, Gabriel A. The Appeals of Communism.
    Princeton: Princeton University Press, 1954.
_____. "Comparative Political Systems," Journal
    of Politics, vol. 18, no. 3 (August 1956), pp.
    391-409.
_____ and James S. Coleman, eds. The Politics
    of the Developing Areas. Princeton: Princeton
    University Press, 1960.
_____ and G. Bingham Powell, Jr. Comparative
    Politics: A Developmental Approach. Boston:
    Little, Brown & Co., 1966.
_____ and Sidney Verba. The Civic Culture: Po-
    litical Attitudes and Democracy in Five Nations.
    Princeton: Princeton University Press, 1963.
Apter, David E., ed. Ideology and Discontent.
    London: Free Press of Glencoe, 1964.
Boorman, Howard L., ed. Biographical Dictionary
    of Republican China, 3 vols. New York: Columbia
    University Press, 1967-70.
Browning, Rufus P. "The Interaction of Personality
    and Political System in Decisions to Run for Of-
    fice: Some Data and a Simulation Technique,"
    Journal of Social Issues, vol. 24, no. 3 (July
    1968), pp. 93-109.
Chang Chi 張繼. Chang P'u-ch'üan hsien-sheng
    ch'üan-chi 張溥泉先生全集 (Collected
    Works of Mr. Chang Chi). Taipei: Chung-yang
    wen-wu kung-ying-she (China Cultural Service),
    October 1951.
_____. Chang P'u-ch'üan hsien-sheng ch'üan-chi
    pu-pien 張溥泉先生全集補編 (Collected
    Works of Mr. Chang Chi: Supplement). Taipei:
    Chung-yang wen-wu kung-ying-she, June 1952.

_____. Chung-kuo Kuo-min-tang shih 中國國民黨史 (A History of the Chinese Kuomintang). Taipei: P'a-mi-erh shu-tien, 1952.

Chang Ch'i-yün 張其昀 . Chung-hua min-kuo shih kang 中華民國史綱 (A General History of the Republic of China), 7 vols. Taipei: Chunghua wen-hua ch'u-pan shih-yeh wei-yüan-hui 中華文化出版事業委員會 (Committee for the Publication of Chinese Cultural Materials), 1954. Published in 1951-52 in five volumes by Chung-yang wen-wu kung-ying-she (China Cultural Service) as Tang-shih kai-yao 黨史概要 (A General History of the Kuomintang).

Chang, H.H. Chiang Kai-shek: Asia's Man of Destiny. Garden City: Doubleday, Doran & Co., 1944.

Ch'en Hsi-hao 陳希豪 . Kuo-ch'ü san-shih-wu nien chung chih Chung-kuo Kuo-min-tang 過去三十五年中之中國國民黨 (The Kuomintang During the Last Thirty-Five Years). Shanghai: The Commercial Press, 1929.

Ch'en Kuo-fu 陳果夫 . Su-cheng hui-i 蘇政回憶 (Reminiscences of the Kiangsu Administration). Taipei: Cheng-chung shu-chü, 1951.

Ch'en Pu-lei 陳布雷 . Ch'en Pu-lei hui-i lu 陳布雷回憶錄 (The Memoirs of Ch'en Pu-lei). Taipei: Chuan-chi wen-hsüeh ch'u-pan-she (Biographical Literature, Inc.), January 1967.

Chen Pu-lai [Ch'en Pu-lei] and Tang Cheng-chu, eds. Chronology of President Chiang Kai-shek. Taipei: China Cultural Service, 1954.

Ch'en Shao-chiao 陳少校 (pseud.). Hei wang lu 黑網錄 (Record of the Black Network). Hong Kong: Chih-ch'eng ch'u-pan-she, 1965.

Cheng Chao 鄭照 et al. Sun Chung-shan hsien-sheng kan-i lu 孫中山先生感憶錄 (Reminiscences Concerning Mr. Sun Yat-sen). Taipei: Wen-hsing shu-tien, 1965.

181

Ch'eng T'ien-fang 程天放. Ch'eng T'ien-fang
tsao-nien hui-i lu 程天放早年回憶錄
(Ch'eng T'ien-fang's Reminiscences of His Early
Years). Taipei: Chuan-chi wen-hsüeh ch'u-pan-
she (Biographical Literature, Inc.), October,
1968.

Cheng Tsung-hsi, Wang An-tsiang, and Wang I-ting.
General Chiang Kai-shek: The Builder of New
China, with an Introduction by Chengting T.
Wang and a Preface by Wang Chung-hui. Shang-
hai: The Commercial Press, 1929.

Cherepanov, A.I. Zapiski Voennogo Sovetnika v
Kitae; iz Istorii Perovi Grazhdanskoi Revolut-
sionnoi Voiny, 1924-1927 (Notes of a Military
Adviser in China; from the History of the First
Revolutionary Civil War in China, 1924-1927),
vol. 1. Moscow: Academy of Sciences of the
USSR, 1964.

Chiang Ching-kuo 蔣經國. Fu-chung chih-yüan
負重致遠 (Carrying a Heavy Burden, Reaching
Toward a Distant Goal). Taipei: Kuo-fang-pu
yin-chih-ch'ang 國防部印製廠 (Ministry
of National Defense, Publication Bureau), 1960.

Chiang Chung-cheng 蔣中正. "Che-hsüeh yü chiao-
yü tui-yü ch'ing-nien ti kuan-hsi" 哲學與教
育對於青年的關係 (The Relevance of Philosophy and Education to Youth), July 9-10, 1941,
in Chiang tsung-t'ung yen-lun hui-pien, vol.
15, pp. 269-95.

_____. "Ch'en Ying-shih hsien-sheng kuei-ch'ou
hou chih ke-ming chi-hua chi shih lüeh" 陳英
士先生癸丑後之革命計劃及事略 (A Summary of
Mr. Ch'en Ch'i-mei's Revolutionary Plans and
Activities Since 1913), in Ho Chung-hsiao, ed.
Ch'en Ying-shih hsien-sheng chi-nien ch'üan-chi,
1:1, 24b-29b; and in Chiang Chung-cheng, Chiang
tsung-t'ung yen-lun hui-pien, vol. 24, pp. 31-
36, dated May 26, 1916.

_____. "Cheng Meng tso-chan ch'u-i" 征蒙作
戰芻議 (Humble Suggestions on a Military Expedition in Mongolia), December 1912, in Tzu-
fan lu, 1:1, 48-80.

_____. "Chi tsung-li wen" 祭總理文 (Funeral
Eulogy for Director [Sun]), March 30, 1925, in
Chiang tsung-t'ung yen-lun hui-pien, vol. 24,
pp. 131-32; also in Mao (A), 9 ts'e, pp. 84b-
86b.

_____. "Chiang Chung-cheng Sung-Hu ch'i-i
chün-shih chi-hua shu" 蔣中正淞滬起義軍事
計劃書 (Chiang Kai-shek's Military Plan for
an Uprising in Woosung-Shanghai), in Lo Chia-
lun, ed., Ke-ming wen-hsien, vol. 6, pp. 770-
76.

_____. Chiang tsung-ts'ai chih yu-jen shu
蔣總裁致友人書 (Director-General Chiang's
Letters to Friends), comp. by Wang Ming-ta
王明達. T'ien-hsia shu-tien, 1941.

_____. Chiang tsung-t'ung yen-lun hui-pien
蔣總統言論彙編 (Collected Speeches and
Messages of President Chiang), 27 vols. Taipei: Cheng-chung shu-chü, October 31, 1956-
October 31, 1959.

_____. "Chün-cheng t'ung-i wen-t'i" 軍政統一
問題 (Questions Concerning the Centralization
of Military Administration), 1912, in Tzu-fan
lu, 1:5, 345-55.

_____. "Chün-sheng tsa-chih fa-k'an-tz'u" 軍
聲雜誌發刊詞 (Foreword to the Military
Voice Magazine), 1912, in Tzu-fan lu, 1:5,
413-17.

_____, comp. Chiang wei-yüan-chang shou-ting
ke-ming shu-chien 蔣委員長手訂革命書簡
(Revolutionary Letters of Chairman Chiang).
Shanghai: Wen-shih yen-chiu-hui, April 1947.

_____. Eulogy for Ch'en Ch'i-mei, May 20,
1916, in Mao (A), 1:5 ts'e, pp. 17a-19a; and in
Ho Chung-hsiao, ed., Ch'en Ying-shih hsien-sheng
chi-nien ch'üan-chi, 1:4, 13a-b.

_____. Eulogy for his maternal grandfather, June 10, 1932, in Mao (A), 1:3 ts'e, pp. 4b-7b.

_____. Eulogy for his maternal grandmother, November 8, 1932, in Mao (A), 1:3 ts'e, pp. 2a-4b.

_____. "Fei-tu ts'ai-ping i" 廢督裁兵議 (On the Abolition of Military Governors and the Disbandment of Troops), February 19, 1919, in Tzu-fan lu, 1:1, 24-26.

_____. "Fu Ku Tzu-ts'ai shu" 復顧子才書 (Reply to Ku Tzu-ts'ai), 1912, in Chiang tsung-t'ung yen-lun hui-pien, vol. 24, pp. 80-81; also in Chung-hua min-kuo k'ai-kuo wu-shih nien wen-hsien pien-tsuan wei-yüan-hui, vol. 4, Ko-sheng kuang-fu, pp. 145-46.

_____. "Fu Liao Chung-k'ai shu" 復廖仲愷書 (Reply to Liao Chung-k'ai), January 26, 1923, in Chiang tsung-t'ung yen-lun hui-pien, vol. 24, pp. 90-92; also in Mao (A), 5 ts'e, pp. 4b-9b.

_____. "Fu Liao Chung-k'ai shu" 復廖仲愷書 (Reply to Liao Chung-k'ai), March 14, 1924, in Chiang tsung-t'ung yen-lun hui-pien, vol. 24, pp. 93-97; also in Mao (A), 6 ts'e, pp. 20b-31a.

_____. "Fu shang tsung-li shu" 復上總理書 (Reply to Director [Sun]), March 2, 1924, in Chiang tsung-t'ung yen-lun hui-pien, vol. 24, pp. 74-79.

_____. "Fu Tai Chi-t'ao shu" 復戴季陶書 (Reply to Tai Chi-t'ao), January 5, 1921, in Chiang tsung-t'ung yen-lun hui-pien, vol. 24, pp. 102-03; also in Mao (A), 3 ts'e, pp. 42b-46b.

_____. "Hsien-pi Wang t'ai-fu-jen shih-lüeh" 先妣王太夫人事略 (A Summary Biography of My Late Mother Wang), June 25, 1921, in Chiang tsung-t'ung yen-lun hui-pien, vol. 24, pp. 63-65; also in Mao (A), 3 ts'e, pp. 77b-83a.

184

_____. "Hui-fu ke-ming ching-shen ho chi-lü" 恢復革命精神和紀律 (Revive Revolutionary Spirit and Discipline), February 11, 1928, in Chiang tsung-t'ung yen-lun hui-pien, vol. 9, pp. 52-55.

_____. "K'an ai-ssu-lu so kan" 刊哀思錄所感 (Thoughts on the Publication of Laments [for My Deceased Mother]), August 19, 1923, in Chiang tsung-t'ung yen-lun hui-pien, vol. 24, p. 67; also in Mao (A), 5 ts'e, pp. 42a-44a.

_____. "Ke-ming chan hou chün-cheng chih ching-ying" 革命戰後軍政之經營 (The Conduct of Military Administration After the Revolutionary War), July 1912, in Tzu-fan lu, 1:5, 319-45.

_____. "K'u mu wen" 哭母文 (Elegy for My Mother), June 15, 1921, in Chiang tsung-t'ung yen-lun hui-pien, vol. 24, pp. 141-42; and in Mao (A), 3 ts'e, pp. 75b-77b.

_____. "Meng-Ts'ang wen-t'i chih ken-pen chieh-chüeh" 蒙藏問題之根本解決 (Fundamental Solutions to the Problems of Mongolia and Tibet), [October?] 1912, in Tzu-fan lu, 1:5, 356-67.

_____. "On the Centennial of the Birth of Dr. Sun Yat-sen," Chung-yang jih-pao (Central Daily News), November 12, 1965, p. 1, for the Chinese text, and November 13, 1965, p. 1, for the English version.

_____. "Pa-erh-kan chan-chü ying-hsiang yü Chung-kuo yü lieh-kuo chih wai-chiao" 巴尔幹戰局影響於中國與列國之外交 (The Effects of the Military Situation in the Balkans on China's Foreign Relations with Other Countries), [November?] 1912, in Tzu-fan lu, 1:5, 368-76.

_____. "Pao-kuo yü ssu-ch'in" 報國與思親 (A Public Message and Some Private Reflections), October 31, 1936, in Chiang tsung-t'ung yen-lun hui-pien, vol. 24, pp. 68-72; translated as

"Some Reflections on My Fiftieth Birthday," in S.I. Hsiung, The Life of Chiang Kai-shek, Appendix 2, pp. 373-78.

_____. "Pen-tang tsui-chin ti chung-yao wen-t'i" 本黨最近的重要問題 (Important Problems of the Party in Recent Years), February 4, 1929, in Tzu-fan lu, 2:15, 1497-1506.

_____. Preface to the First Whampoa Student Directory, April 23, 1925, in Mao (A), 10 ts'e, pp. 26a-32b.

_____. "Some Reflections on My Fiftieth Birthday." See Chiang, "Pao-kuo yü ssu-ch'in."

_____. Soviet Russia in China: A Summing-Up at Seventy. New York: Farrar, Straus & Cudahy, 1957.

_____. Sun ta-tsung-t'ung Kuang-chou meng-nan jih-chi 孫大總統廣州蒙難日記 (A Daily Record of President Sun During the Canton Coup). Shanghai: Min-chih shu-chü, June 1927.

_____. "Tsung-li tui chün-hsiao tsui shen-ch'ieh ti chiao-hsün" 總理對軍校最深切的教訓 (Director Sun's Most Apposite Admonition to the Military Academy), April 5, 1925, in Chiang tsung-t'ung yen-lun hui-pien, vol. 8, 175-77; extracted in Mao (A), 10 ts'e, pp. 3a-4b.

_____. "Tz'u an chi" 慈菴記 (Dedicating a Shrine to My Mother), December 17, 1923, in Mao (A), 5 ts'e, pp. 74b-76b; and in Chiang, Tzu-fan lu, 1:6, 517-18, where the date is erroneously given as 1922.

_____. Tzu-fan lu 自反錄 (Records of Self-Examination), 2 parts. n.p., [1931?].

_____. "Wang ti Jui-ch'ing ai-chuang" 亡弟瑞青哀狀 (A Lament for My Deceased Brother Jui-ch'ing), April 10, 1918, in Tzu-fan lu, 1:6, 438-41.

_____. "Wei Hang-chou kuang-fu chi fu Ku Tzu-ts'ai shu" 為杭州光復記復顧子才書

(Reply to Ku Tzu-ts'ai Concerning <u>An Account of</u>
<u>the Liberation of Hangchow</u>). See Chiang, "Fu
Ku Tzu-ts'ai shu."

_____. "Yü Chang Ching-chiang shu" 與張靜江書
(Letter to Chang Ching-chiang), January 10,
1921, in <u>Chiang Tsung-t'ung yen-lun hui-pien</u>,
vol. 24, p. 101; also in Mao (A), 3 ts'e, pp.
51a-53a.

_____. "Yü Chang P'u-ch'üan shu" 與張溥泉書
(Letter to Chang Chi), in <u>Tzu-fan lu</u>, 1:4, 269.

_____. "Yü Yang Ts'ang-pai shu" 與楊滄白書
(Letter to Yang Shu-k'an), July 13, 1923, in
<u>Chiang tsung-t'ung yen-lun hui-pien</u>, vol. 24,
pp. 105-07.

Chiang Hsing-te 蔣星德 . "Chiang chu-hsi ti tu-
shu sheng-huo" 蔣主席的讀書生活 (Chairman
Chiang's Education), in Li Hsü, ed., <u>Chung-kuo</u>
<u>yü Chiang chu-hsi</u>, pp. 139-46.

_____. "Chu-hsi chih sheng-p'ing" 主席之生平
(The Life of the Chairman), in Teng Wen-i, ed.,
<u>Wei-ta ti Chiang chu-hsi</u>, pp. 56-154.

Chiang Meng-lin 蔣夢麟 . "Chui-i Chung-shan
hsien-sheng" 追憶中山先生 (Reminiscences
Concerning Mr. Sun Yat-sen), in Cheng Chao,
<u>Sun Chung-shan hsien-sheng kan-i lu</u>, pp. 31-35.

Chiang Yung-ching 蔣永敬 . <u>Pao-lo-t'ing yü Wu-</u>
<u>Han cheng-ch'üan</u> 鮑羅廷與武漢政權 (Boro-
din and the Wuhan Regime). Taipei: Chung-kuo
hsüeh-shu chu-tso chiang-chu wei-yüan-hui 中國
學術著作獎助委員會 (China Committee for
Publication Aid and Prize Awards), December
1963.

Chin Ch'eng 金成 . "Chiang Chieh-shih hsien-
sheng chuan lüeh" 蔣介石先生傳略 (A Sum-
mary Biography of Mr. Chiang Kai-shek), Appendix to Chin Ch'eng, ed., <u>Chiang Chung-cheng</u>
<u>ch'üan-chi</u>, vol. 2, pp. 1-6.

_____, ed. <u>Chiang Chung-cheng ch'üan-chi</u> 蔣中
正全集 (The Complete Works of Chiang Kai-shek),

2 vols. Shanghai: Min-tsu ch'u-pan-she,
June 1937.

China Weekly Review (Shanghai), 1917-24.

China Year Book, 1916-28.

Chinese Yearbook (Taipei), 1961-65.

Chow Tse-tsung. The May Fourth Movement: Intellectual Revolution in Modern China. Cambridge:
Harvard University Press, 1960.

Chü Cheng 居正 . Mei-ch'uan jih-chi 梅川日記
(The Diary of Chü Cheng). Shanghai: Ta-tung
shu-chü, September 1947.

_____. Mei-ch'uan p'u-chieh 梅川譜偈 (An
Autobiography in Verse). Privately distributed
by Chang Ming 張鳴 , 1949.

Chu Chih-hsin 朱執信 . Chu Chih-hsin chi 朱
執信集 (Collected Works of Chu Chih-hsin), 2
vols. Shanghai: Min-chih shu-chü, February
1928.

_____. Chu Chih-hsin wen-ch'ao 朱執信文鈔
(Selected Works of Chu Chih-hsin), comp. by
Shao Yüan-ch'ung 邵元冲 . Shanghai: Min-chih
shu-chü, May 1927.

_____. Elegy for Chiang Kai-shek's father, in
Mao (A), 1:1 ts'e, p. 11a-b.

Chung-hua min-kuo k'ai-kuo wu-shih nien wen-hsien
pien-tsuan wei-yüan-hui 中華民國開國五十年
文獻編纂委員會(Committee for the Compila-
tion of Documents on the Fiftieth Anniversary
of the Founding of the Republic of China), ed.
Chung-hua min-kuo k'ai-kuo wu-shih nien wen-
hsien 中華民國開國五十年文獻 (Docu-
ments on the Fiftieth Anniversary of the Founding of the Republic of China), 2nd series. Vol.
3, Hsin-hai ke-ming yü min-kuo chien-yüan 辛亥
革命與民國建元(The 1911 Revolution and
the Founding of the Republic), March 10, 1962.
Vol. 4, Ko-sheng kuang-fu 各省光復 (Liberation of the Various Provinces), May 10, 1962.

188

Chung-kuo Kuo-min-tang chung-yang chih-hsing wei-yüan-hui Yüeh-Min-ch'ü hsüan-ch'uan chuan-yüan pan-kung-ch'u 中國國民黨中央執行委員會 粵閩區宣傳專員辦公處 (Office of the Special Propaganda Officer, Kwangtung-Fukien District, Central Executive Committee of the Kuomintang), ed. Kuo-fu Sun hsien-sheng nien-p'u 國父孫先生年譜 (A Biography of Mr. Sun Yat-sen). n.p., [1939?].

Chung-kuo Kuo-min-tang Kuang-tung sheng chih-hsing wei-yüan-hui 中國國民黨廣東省執行委員會 (Executive Committee of the Kwangtung Provincial Kuomintang), ed. Sun ta-tsung-t'ung Kuang-chou meng-nan shih chou-nien chi-nien chuan-k'an 孫大總統廣州蒙難十週年紀念專刊 (A Special Commemorative Symposium on the Tenth Anniversary of the Canton Coup Against President Sun). [Canton], June 1932.

Chung-yang jih-pao 中央日報 (Central Daily News) (Taipei), 1960-70.

Clark, Elmer T. The Chiangs of China. New York: Abingdon-Cokesbury, 1943.

Coleman, James S., ed. Education and Political Development. Princeton: Princeton University Press, 1965.

Dawson, Richard E. and Kenneth Prewitt. Political Socialization. Boston: Little, Brown & Co., 1969.

Erikson, Erik H. Childhood and Society. New York: W.W. Norton & Co., 1964.

_____. Gandhi's Truth: On the Origins of Militant Nonviolence. New York: W.W. Norton & Co., 1969.

_____. Identity: Youth and Crisis. New York: W.W. Norton & Co., 1968.

_____. Young Man Luther: A Study in Psychoanalysis and History. New York: W.W. Norton & Co., 1958.

189

Fairbank, John K. and Liu Kwang-ching. <u>Modern China: A Bibliographical Guide to Chinese Works</u>. Cambridge: Harvard University Press, 1950.

Feng Han-ming 馮漢明 . "Sui-wei Sun ta-tsung-t'ung ch'u-shih chi" 隨衛孫大總統出師記 (In Attendance on President Sun During the Expedition), in Cheng Chao, <u>Sun Chung-shan hsien-sheng kan-i lu</u>, pp. 79-91.

Feng Tzu-yu 馮自由 . <u>Chung-hua min-kuo k'ai-kuo ch'ien ke-ming shih</u> 中華民國開國前革命史 (A History of the Revolution before the Founding of the Republic of China), 3 vols. Shanghai: Chung-kuo wen-hua fu-wu-she, [May 1944], January 1946.

_____. <u>Chung-hua min-kuo k'ai-kuo ch'ien ke-ming shih hsü-pien</u> 中華民國開國前革命史續編 (A History of the Revolution before the Founding of the Republic of China: Supplement), vol. 1. Shanghai: Chung-kuo wen-hua fu-wu-she, August 1946.

_____. <u>Ke-ming i-shih</u> 革命逸史 (Aspects of the History of the Revolution), 5 vols. Taipei: The Commercial Press, October 1965.

Feuerwerker, Albert, Rhoads Murphey, and Mary C. Wright, eds. <u>Approaches to Modern Chinese History</u>. Berkeley: University of California Press, 1967.

Fischer, Louis. <u>The Soviets in World Affairs: A History of the Relations Between the Soviet Union and the Rest of the World, 1917-1929</u>, 2 vols. 2nd ed., Princeton: Princeton University Press, 1951.

Freud, Anna. <u>The Ego and the Mechanisms of Defense</u>, based upon the translation by Cecil Baines. Rev. ed., New York: International Universities Press, 1966.

Freud, Sigmund. <u>A General Introduction to Psycho-Analysis</u>, trans. by Joan Riviere. New York: Perma Giants, 1949.

Fromm-Reichmann, Frieda. <u>Principles of Intensive Psychotherapy</u>. Chicago: University of Chicago Press, 1950.

Fu Ch'i-hsüeh 傅啟學. <u>Kuo-fu Sun Chung-shan hsien-sheng chuan</u> 國父孫中山先生傳 (A Biography of Mr. Sun Yat-sen, Founding Father of the Republic). Taipei: Chung-hua min-kuo ko-chieh chi-nien kuo-fu pai-nien tan-ch'en ch'ou-pei wei-yüan-hui 中華民國各界紀念國父百年誕辰籌備委員會 (Preparatory Committee of Various Circles in the Republic of China to Commemorate the Hundredth Anniversary of the Birth of the Founding Father), November 1965.

George, Alexander L. "Comments on [M. Brewster Smith's] 'Opinions, Personality, and Political Behavior,'" <u>American Political Science Review</u>, vol. 52, no. 1 (March 1958), pp. 18-26.

_____. "Power as a Compensatory Value for Political Leaders," <u>Journal of Social Issues</u>, vol. 24, no. 3 (July 1968), pp. 29-49.

_____ and Juliette L. George. <u>Woodrow Wilson and Colonel House: A Personality Study</u>. New York: John Day Co., 1956.

Gibbons, David S. "Dominant Political Leadership and Political Integration in a Transitional Society: China, Chiang Kai-shek and Mao Tsetung, 1935-1949," Ph.D. dissertation, Princeton University, 1968.

Greenstein, Fred I. "The Impact of Personality on Politics: An Attempt to Clear Away Underbrush," <u>American Political Science Review</u>, vol. 61, no. 3 (September 1967), pp. 629-41.

_____. <u>Personality and Politics: Problems of Evidence, Inference, and Conceptualization</u>. Chicago: Markham Publishing Co., 1969.

_____. "Personality and Politics: Problems of Evidence, Inference, and Conceptualization," in Seymour Martin Lipset, ed., <u>Politics and the Social Sciences</u> (New York: Oxford University Press, 1969), pp. 163-206.

Hackett, Roger F. "Chinese Students in Japan, 1900-1910," Papers on China (Cambridge: Committee on International and Regional Studies, Harvard University), vol. 3, May 1949, pp. 134-69.

Hahn, Emily. Chiang Kai-shek: An Unauthorized Biography. New York: Doubleday & Co., 1955.

_____. The Soong Sisters. New York: Doubleday, Doran & Co., 1941.

Ho Chung-hsiao 何仲簫 , ed. Ch'en Ying-shih hsien-sheng chi-nien ch'üan-chi 陳英士先生紀念全集 (Collected Works in Commemoration of Mr. Ch'en Ch'i-mei). n.p., [1930?].

_____. Ch'en Ying-shih hsien-sheng nien-p'u 陳英士先生年譜 (A Biography of Mr. Ch'en Ch'i-mei). Shanghai: Chung-kuo wen-hua fu-wu-she, April 1946.

_____. "Nien-p'u ch'u-kao" 年譜初稿 (Preliminary Draft of a Biography [of Ch'en Ch'i-mei]), in Ch'en Ying-shih hsien-sheng chi-nien ch'üan-chi, 1:1, 1a-7b.

Horney, Karen. Our Inner Conflict: A Constructive Theory of Neurosis. New York: W.W. Norton & Co., 1945, 1966.

Hsieh Chung-san 薛仲三 and Ou-yang I 歐陽頤 , comps. Liang-ch'ien nien Chung-Hsi li tui-chao piao 兩千年中西曆對照表 (A Sino-Western Calendar for Two Thousand Years, 1-2000 A.D.). Hong Kong: The Commercial Press, July 1961.

Hsiung, S.I. The Life of Chiang Kai-shek. London: Peter Davies, 1948.

Hsü, Leonard S. Sun Yat-sen: His Political and Social Ideals. Los Angeles: University of Southern California Press, 1933.

Hsü T'ang 徐棠 . Hsin-hai kan-ssu-t'uan yüan-ch'i yü Hu chün-shih ke-ming shih-lüeh 辛亥敢死團緣起與滬軍事革命史略 (The Origin of the 1911 Dare-to-Die Corps and a Brief History of the Military Revolution in Shanghai) ex-

tracted in Chung-hua min-kuo k'ai-kuo wu-shih
nien wen-hsien pien-tsuan wei-yüan-hui, ed.,
vol. 3, <u>Hsin-hai ke-ming yü min-kuo chien-yüan</u>,
pp. 365-69.

Hu Ch'ü-fei 胡去非. <u>Sun Chung-shan hsien-sheng
chuan</u> 孫中山先生傳 (A Biography of Mr. Sun
Yat-sen). Shanghai: The Commercial Press, March
1933.

_____. <u>Tsung-li shih lüeh</u> 總理事略(A Brief
Account of the Activities of Director [Sun]).
Shanghai: The Commercial Press, October 1937.

Hu Han-min 胡漢民. "Liu yüeh shih-liu hui-ku"
六月十六迴顧 (Reminiscences About June 16),
in Chung-kuo Kuo-min-tang Kuang-tung sheng chih-
hsing wei-yüan-hui, ed., <u>Sun ta-tsung-t'ung
Kuang-chou meng-nan shih chou-nien chi-nien
chuan-k'an</u>, pp. 15-26.

_____. "Tsung-li Kuang-chou meng-nan ching-
kuo" 總理廣州蒙難經過(Director [Sun]
During the Canton Coup), [1930], in Chung-kuo
Kuo-min-tang Kuang-tung sheng chih-hsing wei-
yüan-hui, ed., pp. 27-33.

Hu Wen-ts'an 胡文燦. "Sun ta-tsung-t'ung
Kuang-chou meng-nan shih li-chien kuo-Hu chi-
shu" 孫大總統廣州蒙難時離艦過滬紀述
(An Account of President Sun's Departure from
the Fleet for Shanghai During the Canton Coup),
in Chung-kuo Kuo-min-tang Kuang-tung sheng chih-
hsing wei-yüan-hui, ed., p. 42.

Hua Lin-i 華林一. <u>Chung-kuo Kuo-min-tang shih</u>
中國國民黨史 (A History of the Kuomin-
tang), ed. by Ts'ai Yüan-p'ei 蔡元培.
Shanghai: The Commercial Press, June 1928.

Huang Chi-lu 黃季陸. "Kuo-fu shih-shih ch'ien
hou" 國父逝世前後(Before and After the
Death of the Founding Father of the Republic),
in Cheng Chao et al., <u>Sun Chung-shan hsien-
sheng kan-i lu</u>, pp. 141-60.

Huang Chieh 黃杰 . Chiang Chieh-shih hsien-sheng
chuan chi 蔣介石先生傳記 (A Biography of
Mr. Chiang Kai-shek). Shanghai: Chung-yung shu-
tien, 1937.

Huang Hui-lung 黃惠龍 . Chung-shan hsien-sheng
ch'in-cheng lu 中山先生親征錄 (An Account
of the Personal Expedition of Mr. Sun), recorded by Ch'en T'ieh-sheng 陳鉄生 . Shanghai: The Commercial Press, August 1930.

Hyman, Herbert H. Political Socialization: A
Study in the Psychology of Political Behavior.
Glencoe: The Free Press, 1959.

Ishimaru Tōta 石丸藤太 . Chiang Chieh-shih
chuan 蔣介石傳 (A Biography of Chiang Kai-
shek), trans. by Shih Lo-ying 施落英 .
Shanghai: Kuang-hua ch'u-pan-she, 1937.

Jansen, Marius B. The Japanese and Sun Yat-sen.
Cambridge: Harvard University Press, 1954.

Johnson, Chalmers A. "The Role of Social Science
in China Scholarship," World Politics, vol. 17,
no. 2 (January 1965), pp. 256-71.

Kao Yin-tsu 高蔭祖 . Kuo-fu nien-piao chien-
pien 國父年表簡編 (A Short Chronological
Biography of the Founding Father of the Republic). [Taipei?]: Chung-hua min-kuo ta-shih-chi
pien-i-she, November 1966.

Ku Ying-fen 古應芬 . Min-kuo shih-erh nien Sun
ta-yüan-shuai tung-cheng jih-chi 民國十二年
孫大元帥東征日記 (Diary of Generalissi-
mo Sun's Eastern Expedition in 1923). Shanghai: Min-chih shu-chü, November 1926.

Kuo-fang ch'u-pan-she 國防出版社 , ed. Wei-ta
ti Chiang chu-hsi 偉大的蔣主席 (The Illustrious Chairman Chiang). Hong Kong: Pai-ling-
hang, 1946.

Kuo-min chiu-kuo hui 國民救國會 , ed. Chiang
Chieh-shih Ch'en Chi-t'ang mai-kuo yang-min i-
p'ieh 蔣介石陳濟棠賣國殃民一瞥
(Chiang Kai-shek and Ch'en Chi-t'ang: A Look at
Their Treason and Oppressive Rule). n.p., 1933.

194

Kuo T'ing-i 郭廷以. Chin-tai Chung-kuo shih-
shih jih-chih Ch'ing-chi 近代中國史事日
誌：清季 (A Chronology of Modern Chinese His-
tory: The Late Ch'ing Period), 2 vols. Taipei:
Cheng-chung shu-chü, 1963.
Lane, Robert E. Political Ideology: Why the Ameri-
can Common Man Believes What He Does. New York:
The Free Press, 1962.
_____. Political Thinking and Consciousness:
The Private Life of the Political Mind. Chi-
cago: Markham Publishing Co., 1969.
Langton, Kenneth P. Political Socialization. New
York: Oxford University Press, 1969.
Lasswell, Harold D. Politics: Who Gets What, When,
How. Cleveland: World Publishing Co., 1958.
_____. Power and Personality. New York: W.W.
Norton & Co., 1948.
_____. Psychopathology and Politics. Chica-
go: University of Chicago Press, 1930.
Li Chien-nung. The Political History of China,
1840-1928, trans. & ed. by Ssu-yu Teng and
Jeremy Ingalls. Princeton: D. Van Nostrand
Co., 1956.
Li Hsü 李旭, ed. Liu-shih nien lai ti Chung-
kuo yü Chiang chu-hsi 六十年來的中國與
蔣主席 (China and Chairman Chiang During the
Last Sixty Years). Nanking: Pa-t'i shu-chü,
1946.
Li Tsung-jen. "The Reminiscences of General Li
Tsung-jen," as recorded by T.K. Tong. Unpub-
lished manuscript, dated December 1, 1964,
Chinese Oral History Project, East Asian Insti-
tute, Columbia University.
Li Yün-han 李雲漢. Ts'ung jung-kung tao ch'ing
tang 從容共到清黨 (From Kuomintang-Commu-
nist Coalition to Party Purification), 2 vols.
Taipei: Chung-kuo hsüeh-shu chu-tso chiang-chu
wei-yüan-hui 中國學術著作獎助委員會
(China Committee for Publication Aid and Prize
Awards), 1966.
195

Liang Chung-ming 梁中銘 . <u>Chiang chu-hsi hua-
chuan</u> 蔣主席畫傳 (An Illustrated Biography
of Chairman Chiang). [Shanghai]: Cheng-ch'i
ch'u-pan-she, 1947.

_____ et al. <u>Wei-ta ti Chiang chu-hsi</u> 偉大的
蔣主席 (The Illustrious Chairman Chiang). Kuo-
fang-pu hsin-wen chü 國防部新聞局 (News
Bureau, Ministry of National Defense), 1946.

Liang Lieh-ya 梁烈亞 . "Kuo-fu i-shih t'an" 國父
逸事談 (Reminiscences of Extraordinary Events
Concerning the Founding Father of the Republic),
in Cheng Chao, <u>Sun Chung-shan hsien-sheng kan-i
lu</u>, pp. 177-84.

Lifton, Robert J. <u>Revolutionary Immortality: Mao
Tse-tung and the Chinese Revolution</u>. New York:
Random House, 1968.

Lin Chih-mien 林直勉 and Chao Kuei-chang 招桂章
"Sun ta-tsung-t'ung meng-nan chi kang-mu" 孫大
總統蒙難記綱目 (An Outline of the Coup
Against President Sun), in Chung-kuo Kuo-min-
tang Kuang-tung sheng chih-hsing wei-yüan-hui,
pp. 57-66.

Linebarger, Paul M.A. <u>The China of Chiang K'ai-
shek: A Political Study</u>. Boston: World Peace
Foundation, 1941.

Liu, F.F. <u>A Military History of Modern China,
1924-1949</u>. Princeton: Princeton University
Press, 1956.

Lo Chia-lun 羅家倫 . <u>Ch'i-shih nien lai chih
Chung-kuo Kuo-min-tang yü Chung-kuo</u> 七十年來之
中國國民黨與中國 (The Kuomintang and
China, 1895-1964). Taichung: Chung-kuo Kuo-
min-tang chung-yang wei-yüan-hui tang-shih
shih-liao pien-tsuan wei-yüan-hui 中國國民
黨中央委員會黨史史料編纂委員會 (Commis-
sion for Compiling Historical Documents of the
Party, Central Executive Committee of the Kuomintang), November 24, 1964.

_____, ed. <u>Ke-ming wen-hsien</u> 革命文獻 (Documents of the Revolution), 43 vols. Taichung: Chung-kuo Kuo-min-tang chung-yang wei-yüan-hui tang-shih shih-liao pien-tsuan wei-yüan-hui 中國國民黨中央委員會黨史史料編纂委員會 (Commission for Compiling Historical Documents of the Party, Central Executive Committee of the Kuomintang), 1953-March 1968.

_____. <u>Kuo-fu nien-p'u erh-kao</u> 國父年譜二稿 (A Chronological Biography of the Founding Father of the Republic, Second Draft), 2 vols. n.p., n.d.

_____. <u>Liu-shih nien lai chih Chung-kuo Kuo-min-tang yü Chung-kuo</u> 六十年來之中國國民黨與中國 (The Kuomintang and China, 1895-1954). Chung-kuo Kuo-min-tang chung-yang wei-yüan-hui ti-ssu tsu tang-shih shih-liao pien-tsuan wei-yüan-hui 中國國民黨中央委員會第四組黨史史料編纂委員會 (Central Executive Committee of the Kuomintang, Fourth Section, Commission for Compiling Historical Documents of the Party), November 1954.

Loh, Pichon P.Y. "The Ideological Persuasion of Chiang Kai-shek," <u>Modern Asian Studies</u> (London), vol. 4, part 3 (July 1970), pp. 211-38.

_____, ed. <u>The Kuomintang Debacle of 1949: Conquest or Collapse?</u> Boston: D.C. Heath, 1965.

_____. "The Politics of Chiang Kai-shek: A Reappraisal," <u>Journal of Asian Studies</u>, vol. 25, no. 3 (May 1966), pp. 431-51.

_____. "The Politics of Chiang Kai-shek: His Policy of Unity," a paper presented to the University Seminar on Modern East Asia: China, Columbia University, February 21, 1968.

MacFarquhar, Roderick L. "The Whampoa Military Academy," <u>Papers on China</u> (Cambridge: Committee on International and Regional Studies, Harvard University), vol. 9 (1955), pp. 146-72.

197

McClosky, Herbert. "Conservatism and Personality,"
American Political Science Review, vol. 52, no.
1 (March 1958), pp. 27-45.

Mao Ssu-ch'eng 毛 思 誠 . Min-kuo shih-wu nien i-
ch'ien chih Chiang Chieh-shih hsien-sheng
民國十五年以前之蔣介石先生 (Mr. Chiang
Kai-shek, 1887-1926). Hong Kong: Lung-men shu-
tien, [October 1936], November 1965. Referred
to as Mao (A).

_____ . Min-kuo shih-wu nien i-ch'ien chih
Chiang Chieh-shih hsien-sheng, ed. by Ch'en Pu-
lei 陳布雷 , 2 vols. n.p., n.d. Referred to
as Mao (B).

_____ . "Min-kuo yüan-nien ch'ien chih Chiang
Chieh-shih hsien-sheng" 民國元年前之蔣介石
先生 (Mr. Chiang Kai-shek, 1887-1911), in
Teng Wen-i, ed., Wei-ta ti Chiang chu-hsi, pp.
44-51. Referred to as Mao (C).

New York Times, 1924-27.

North, Robert C. Moscow and Chinese Communists.
2nd ed., Stanford: Stanford University Press,
1963.

Palmer, Norman D. "Makers of Modern China: V, The
Generalissimo: Chiang Kai-shek," Current History, vol. 15, no. 88 (December 1948), pp. 338-
41.

_____ . "Makers of Modern China: VI, Chiang
Kai-shek: Immovable Stone," Current History,
vol. 15, no. 89 (January 1949), pp. 1-6.

P'an Kung-chan 潘公展 . Ch'en Ch'i-mei 陳其美 .
Taipei: Sheng-li ch'u-pan kung-ssu, 1954.

Payne, Robert. Chiang Kai-shek. New York: Wey-
bright and Talley, 1969.

Powell, Ralph L. The Rise of Chinese Military
Power, 1895-1912. Princeton: Princeton University Press, 1955.

Prewitt, Kenneth. "Political Socialization and
Leadership Selection," The Annals of the American Academy of Political and Social Science,
vol. 361 (September 1965), pp. 96-111.

Pye, Lucian W. Aspects of Political Development.
Boston: Little, Brown & Co., 1966.
_____. Politics, Personality, and Nation-
Building: Burma's Search for Identity. New
Haven: Yale University Press, 1962.
_____. The Spirit of Chinese Politics: A Psy-
chocultural Study of the Authority Crisis in
Political Development. Cambridge: The M.I.T.
Press, 1968.
_____ and Sidney Verba, eds. Political Culture
and Political Development. Princeton: Prince-
ton University Press, 1965.
Rogow, Arnold A. James Forrestal: A Study of
Personality, Politics, and Policy. New York:
Macmillan Co., 1963.
Scalapino, Robert. "Prelude to Marxism: The Chi-
nese Student Movement in Japan, 1900-1910," in
Albert Feuerwerker, Rhoads Murphey, and Mary C.
Wright, eds., Approaches to Modern Chinese His-
tory, pp. 190-215.
Schiffrin, Harold Z. Sun Yat-sen and the Origins
of the Chinese Revolution. Berkeley: University of California Press, 1968.
Shao Yüan-ch'ung 邵元沖. "Chao-ho chan-yü
shih-chi" 肇和戰役實記 (A True Record of
the Battle of the S.S. Chao-ho) in Ho Chung-
hsiao, ed., Ch'en Ying-shih hsien-sheng chi-
nien ch'üan-chi, 1:1, 29b-34b.
_____. Ch'en Ying-shih hsien-sheng ke-ming
hsiao-shih 陳英士先生革命小史 (A Brief
Record of the Revolutionary Career of Mr.
Ch'en Ch'i-mei). Shanghai: Min-chih shu-chü,
[1925?].
_____. "Hsing-chuang" 行狀 (A Brief Biography
[of Ch'en Ch'i-mei]), in Ho Chung-hsiao, Ch'en
Ying-shih hsien-sheng nien-p'u, pp. 76-84.
Sharmon, Lyon. Sun Yat-sen, His Life and Its
Meaning: A Critical Biography. Hamden: Archon
Books, [1934], 1965.

199

Shen I-yün 沈亦雲. I-yün hui-i 亦雲回憶 (Memoirs of Mrs. Huang Fu), 2 vols. Taipei: Biographical Literature, Inc., April 1, 1968.

Sié, Chéou-kang. President Chiang Kai-shek: His Childhood and Youth. Taipei: China Cultural Service, [1954].

Singer, J. David. "Man and World Politics: The Psycho-Cultural Interface," Journal of Social Issues, vol. 24, no. 3 (July 1968), pp. 127-56.

Smelser, Neil J. "Personality and the Explanation of Political Phenomena at the Social-System Level: A Methodological Statement," Journal of Social Issues, vol. 24, no. 3 (July 1968), pp. 111-25.

Smith, M. Brewster. "A Map for the Analysis of Personality and Politics," Journal of Social Issues, vol. 24, no. 3 (July 1968), pp. 15-28.

_____. "Opinions, Personality, and Political Behavior," American Political Science Review, vol. 52, no. 1 (March 1958), pp. 1-26.

_____, Jerome S. Bruner, and Robert W. White. Opinions and Personality. New York: John Wiley & Sons, Inc., 1956.

Sokolsky, George E. "The Kuomintang," China Year Book, 1929-30, pp. 1157-1216.

Stuart, J. Leighton. Fifty Years in China: The Memoirs of John Leighton Stuart. New York: Random House, 1954.

Sun Chung-shan 孫中山. Eulogy for Chiang Kai-shek's deceased mother, November 21, 1921, in Kuo-fu ch'üan-shu, p. 1052; also in Mao (A), 3 ts'e, pp. 95b-96b.

_____. Kuo-fu ch'üan-shu 國父全書 (Complete Works of the Founding Father of the Republic), comp. by Chang Ch'i-yün 張其昀. Taipei: Kuo-fang yen-chiu-yüan 國防研究院 (Institute of National Defense), 1960.

[Tai] Chi-t'ao 戴季陶. "Huai Chu Chih-hsin hsien-sheng" 懷朱執信先生 (Reminiscing About

Mr. Chu Chih-hsin), in Chu, <u>Chu Chih-hsin wen-</u>
<u>ch'ao</u>, pp. 431-39.

_____. <u>Tai Chi-t'ao hsien-sheng wen-ts'un</u>
戴季陶先生文存 (Collected Works of Mr. Tai
Chi-t'ao), comp. by Ch'en T'ien-hsi 陳天錫,
4 vols. Taipei: Kuo-min-tang chung-yang chih-
hsing wei-yüan-hui 國民黨中央執行委員會
(Central Executive Committee of the Kuomintang),
1959.

_____. <u>Tai Chi-t'ao hsien-sheng wen-ts'un hsü-</u>
<u>pien</u> 戴季陶先生文存續編 (Collected Works of
Mr. Tai Chi-t'ao, Supplement), comp. by Ch'en
T'ien-hsi 陳天錫. Taipei: Chung-kuo Kuo-min-
tang chung-yang wei-yüan-hui tang-shih shih-
liao pien-tsuan wei-yüan-hui 中國國民黨中央
委員會黨史史料編纂委員會 (Commission
for Compiling Historical Documents of the Party, Central Executive Committee of the Kuomintang), 1967.

T'ang-jen 唐人 (pseud.). <u>Chin-ling ch'un-meng</u>
金陵春夢 (Dreams and Fancies in Nanking),
with a Preface by Fei I-min 費彝民, 4 vols.
Hong Kong: Yang Yung 楊鏞, [1955], 1966.

T'ang Leang-li. <u>The Inner History of the Chinese</u>
<u>Revolution</u>. London: George Routledge & Sons,
1930.

T'ao Pai-ch'uan 陶百川, ed. <u>Chiang chu-hsi ti</u>
<u>sheng-huo ho sheng-huo-kuan</u> 蔣主席的生活和
生活觀 (Chairman Chiang: His Life and Philosophy of Life). Chungking: Chung-chou ch'u-pan-
she, 1944.

Teng Wen-i 鄧文儀. <u>Chiang chu-hsi</u> 蔣主席 (Chairman Chiang). Shanghai: Sheng-li ch'u-pan-she,
1945.

_____. <u>Chiang chu-hsi chuan-lüeh</u> 蔣主席傳略
(A Brief Biography of Chairman Chiang). Kuo-
fang-pu hsin-wen-chü 國防部新聞局 (News
Bureau, Ministry of National Defense), 1946.

_____, ed. Wei-ta ti Chiang chu-hsi 偉大的蔣
主席 (The Illustrious Chairman Chiang). Kuo-
fang-pu hsin-wen-chü 國防部新聞局 (News
Bureau, Ministry of National Defense), 1946.
Tong, Hollington K. Chiang Kai-shek. Taipei:
China Publishing Co., 1953.
_____. Chiang Kai-shek: Soldier and States-
man, 2 vols. Shanghai: China Publishing Co.,
1937.
Tsou Lu 鄒魯. Chung-kuo Kuo-min-tang shih kao
中國國民黨史稿 (A Draft History of the
Kuomintang), 3 vols. Taipei: The Commercial
Press, 1965.
Tsou, Tang. America's Failure in China, 1941-50.
Chicago: University of Chicago Press, 1963.
"Tsung-li chi Chung-kuo Kuo-min-tang kuan-yü ch'u-
li shang-t'uan shih-pien chih wen-chien" 總理
及中國國民黨關於處理商團事變之文件
(Documents Relating to the Disposition of the
Merchant Corps Incident by Director [Sun] and
the Kuomintang), in Lo Chia-lun, ed., Ke-ming
wen-hsien, vol. 10 (1955), pp. 1473-83.
Tucker, Robert C. "The Dictator and Totalitarian-
ism," World Politics, vol. 17, no. 4 (July
1965), pp. 555-83.
Tung-fang tsa-chih 東方雜誌(The Eastern Miscellany) (Shanghai), 1908-16.
U.S. Department of State. Papers Relating to the
Foreign Relations of the United States, 1927-
1930. Washington, D.C.: U.S. Government Print-
ing Office, 1942-45.
U.S. National Archives. Records of the Department
of State Relating to Internal Affairs of China,
1910-29. Washington, D.C.: National Archives
and Records Service, General Administrative
Service, 1967. Microcopy No. 329.
Wang Ching-wei 汪精衛. "Chih-hsin ti jen-ke"
執信的人格(The Character of Chu Chih-hsin),
in Chu, Chu Chih-hsin wen-ch'ao, pp. 441-48.

Wang Kuan-ying 王冠英. <u>Chiang tsung-t'ung yü
Chung-kuo 蔣總統與中國</u> (President Chiang and
China). Hong Kong: Hua-nan shu-chü, May 1966.

Wang, Y.C. <u>Chinese Intellectuals and the West,
1872-1949</u>. Chapel Hill: University of North
Carolina Press, 1966.

_____. "Tu Yueh-sheng (1888-1951): A Tentative
Political Biography," <u>Journal of Asian Studies</u>,
vol. 26, no. 3 (May 1967), pp. 433-55.

Wen-hua li-chin-she 文化勵進社 (Society for the
Advancement of Culture), ed. <u>Chiang wei-yüan-
chang chuan 蔣委員長傳</u> (A Biography of
Chairman Chiang). Shanghai: Tso-hsin shu-tien,
May 1937.

White, Robert W. <u>The Abnormal Personality</u>. New
York: Ronald Press Co., 1948.

Whiting, Allen S. <u>Soviet Policies in China, 1917-
1924</u>. New York: Columbia University Press,
1953.

Wilbur, C. Martin and Julie Lien-ying How, eds.
<u>Documents on Communism, Nationalism, and Soviet
Advisers in China, 1918-1927</u>. New York: Columbia University Press, 1956.

Wolfenstein, E. Victor. <u>The Revolutionary Personality: Lenin, Trotsky and Gandhi</u>. Princeton:
Princeton University Press, 1967.

Wu, Eugene. <u>Leaders of Twentieth Century China: An
Annotated Bibliography of Selected Chinese Bio-
graphical Works in the Hoover Library</u>. Stanford:
Stanford University Press, 1956.

Wu Hsiang-hsiang 吳相湘. <u>Min-kuo cheng-chih
jen-wu 民國政治人物</u> (Men Who Shaped the Republic), 2 vols. Taipei: Wen-hsing shu-tien,
1966.

Wu I-chou 吳一舟. <u>Chiang Tsung-t'ung hsing-i
蔣總統行誼</u> (The Righteous Life of President
Chiang). Taipei: Cheng-chung shu-chü, 1954.

Yao Yü-hsiang 姚漁湘 et al. Yen-chiu Sun Chung-shan ti shih-liao 研究孫中山的史料 (Historical Data Concerning Sun Yat-sen). Taipei: Wen-hsing shu-tien, 1965.

Young, C.W.H. New Life for Kiangsi, with a Fore-word by Madame Chiang Kai-shek. Shanghai, 1935.

Yu, George T. Party Politics in Republican China: The Kuomintang, 1912-1924. Berkeley: University of California Press, 1966.

INDEX

205

sonality, 12-13, 99; "red-faced general" and
student protest, 16, 22, 104; desirous of great
achievement, 16; disgusted with local officials
and kinfolk, 16; desirous of revolution and new
knowledge, 17; dreams, 19, 20, 49, 50, 69; propensity for order, 21; regulated and purposive
life, 21, 62-63; rebellion against unjust authority, 22; life of intense dissipation, 24-26;
violent temper, 25, 32, 35, 37-38, 39, 40, 44,
64; self-opinionated, 25; summary treatment of
political enemies, 26; sense of persecution, 29,
37-38, 42, 43, 51, 61, 63, 115-16; often wary,
30; given to lust, 32; uncompromising, 32, 35,
72; impulsive, 32, 42, 51; eager to make proposals, 32; nervous strain, 33, 68-69; jealousy
and prejudice, fear of, 35, 43-44, 64, 69, 76,
86, 93; explosive altercation with Tai, 36-37;
ashamed of self, 38; self-control, lacking in,
38, 64; self-willed and incorrigible, 39, 51;
state of intoxication, 39; externalizing feelings, 41; narrow-minded, 42, 56, 65; dignity,
42, 43; desire for clear-cut and fundamental
solutions, 42, 44, 66, 84, 104; goes to extremes, 44, 89, 100; pushes his interests as far
as possible, 47, 85; extremely irritated, 50;
psychological disequilibrium, 51; Ch'en Ch'i-mei
as hero model, 51-52; Tseng Kuo-fan, identification with, 52; misanthropic predisposition, 56;
obsessional-compulsive personality, 56; contemplation and meditation, 56-57, 59-60, 62; remorse, 56-57, 59; self-reliance, 59, 64, 67;
introversion, 59-60; avoidance of confusion
and anxiety, 59, 62; obedience to authority, 60;
avoidance of evil, 60; object appraisal, 61; belief in prophetic nature of dreams, 61; unbounded
faith in himself, 61-62, 102; illustrious throughout the world, 62, 65; acts according to instincts, 143; feelings of guilt, 63; thoughts of
suicide, 63; fulfillment of heaven's will, 63;

207

bores, people as, 64, 104; light-mindedness, 64;
archaic and doltish, 64-65; straightforwardness,
66, 104; universalistic orientation, 66; and incompatible political elements, 74; social events,
noninvolvement in, 75; very bad state of mind,
76; fortitude and persistence, Sun's counsel of,
77; problems in dealing with friends, 86-87;
habit of violence, 87; need to act summarily
without interference, 87; conservative orientation, 92, 106; desirous of personal power and
public service, 92, 100; driven, 92; loyal and
sincere, 92; confidence and trust in him, desirous of, 93, 94; stay if compatible, leave if
not compatible, 94, 95; to work with peace of
mind, 95; admonition to refrain from having too
many opinions, 95; strong ego defense mechanisms,
102; dominant attitude of moving against people,
158-65; integrity crisis, 103, 167; involvement
in action, 96, 104; self-diagnosis disclosed,
105; secular mode of operation, 105; detachment
and objectivity, 106

politics, 134-35, 136, 137, 138-39, 145, 149;
commandant of Whampoa Military Academy, 3, 96,
97, 99; schooling, 14-17, 52, 115, 116; civil
service examination, failure in, 15, 22; instruction on ceremonies, 15; studies English, 16, 58;
prepares himself for military career, 17-20, 21,
52, 120; trips to Japan, 17, 19, 27, 28, 31, 32,
52, 56, 118-19; and Ch'en Ch'i-mei, 19, 22, 24,
25, 26, 27, 29, 121-22, 129, 131; Japanese language, 19; membership in T'ung-meng-hui claimed,
19, 122-23; introduced to Sun, 19-20, 124-25;
involved with revolutionary movement, 20; "de-
vours" Ke-ming chün, 20, 22, 52, 125; li as a
value, 21; to Shanghai in October 1911, 24, 26;
liberation of Hangchow, 26; liquidates T'ao
Ch'eng-chang, 26-27, 52, 104, 128, 134; kills
Ch'en Shun, 128; Military Voice Magazine, 27, 53;
Second Revolution of 1913, 27, 128; membership in

integrity crisis, 103, 165-69
Japan, 54
Jen Chieh-mei, 10
Joffe, Adolf, 73, 87, 147-48, 151; arrives in Peking, 73; joint manifesto with Sun, 78
Karakhan, Leo, 88
Kiangnan Arsenal, 27, 131
Kiangyin Fortress, 29, 130-31
Ku Ch'ing-lien, 16
Ku Ying-fen, 47, 67, 68, 84, 88, 146
Kuomintang, party leaders demand Chiang's services, 60-61, 65, 105-06; reorganization, 73, 77-78, 149; consensus of party leadership, 82; unreliability of warlord armies, 83; Kuomintang-Soviet collaboration, 87-88, 151-53; First National Congress, 91; universalistic orientation, 105; specific and disciplined military training, need for, 105; united front, 106
Kuomintang Archives, 1
Kwangtung, peculiar atmosphere, 43; not a suitable place for Chiang, 46, 47; Chiang's aversion to political environment in, 70; as source of power for Kuomintang, 86
Lasswell, Harold D., 126
legitimacy, Chiang's claim as Sun's successor, 72
Lenin, 88
Li Chi-shen, 88
Li Fu-lin, 146
Li Lieh-chün, 80, 146
Li Tsung-jen, 1, 109
Li Yang-ching, 146
Liao Chung-k'ai, 1, 33, 47, 48, 67, 69, 70, 75, 76, 78, 81, 83, 84, 85, 89, 90, 95, 96, 105, 128, 134, 145, 155; detained by Ch'en Chiung-ming, 146; departs for Japan, 74; governor of Kwangtung, 86, 89, 94, 151, 154; and Joffe, 151; designated head of Whampoa's Political Department, 90; administrative ability questioned, 95; exasperated reply to Chiang, 96; member of Revolutionary Committee, 156
212

Revolutionary Committee, 97, 98, 106, 156
Russia, imperialist designs in Mongolia and Man-
churia, 54; principal aggressor in China, 55
Schiffrin, Harold Z., 119
Second Revolution, 28
secret societies, 24
Shao Yüan-ch'ung, 46, 50, 130, 138-39; dislike for
Ch'en Chiung-ming, 138-39
Shen Hung-ying, 82, 83, 84; revolt of, 85-86
Shen Ting-i, 88
Shimbu Gakkō, 19
Sian coup, 29, 131, 139
Singer, J. David, 110
Smelser, Neil J., 110
Stuart, J. Leighton, 25-26
Sun Hung-i, 80
Sun K'o, administrative ability questioned, 95
Sun-tzu ping-fa, 16, 52
Sun Yat-sen, 1, 16, 29, 31, 33, 35, 45, 46, 47, 48,
49, 50, 51, 57, 59, 64, 66, 105, 118, 130, 136,
137, 148, 149, 151; leaves for Canton in July
1917, 30; generalissimo of Military Government,
30, 134; Chiang's conduct, admonition of, 34-35,
77; opinion of Chu Chih-hsin, 136; departs for
Canton in November 1920, 36; magnanimity of, perceived by Tai, 38, 40-41; straightforwardness of,
perceived by Chiang, 41-43, 51; as constitutional
president in 1921, 139-40; active interest in
Chiang, 66-101, 150; and Chiang's mother, 66-67,
143-44; in uneasy alliance with Ch'en Chiung-
ming, 69; headquarters at Shaokuan, 69-70; escape to warships, 70-72, 145-46; joint manifesto
with Joffe, 78, 87; arrives in Hong Kong in January 1923, 83; search for Soviet assistance, 151-
53; Leo Karakhan, letter to, 88-89; eastern expedition, 89; chairman of Revolutionary Committee, 156; Soviet Union as revolutionary model,
97; disgust with Chiang's recalcitrance, 98;
departs for Peking in November 1924, 99; stops
over at Whampoa, 99-100, 157; death, 156

Tai Chi-t'ao, 32, 33, 36, 46, 48, 51, 71, 83, 90, 105, 134, 137, 155; on Kuomintang "progressing steadily," 38-39, 40-41; persuades Chiang to go to Canton, 39-45; prejudice and sentimentality, 41, 43, 46, 51; sharpness of words, 41, 42-43
Taiping Rebellion, 4, 58, 103-04
T'an P'ing-shan, member of Revolutionary Committee, 156
T'an Yen-k'ai, 80
T'ang Leang-li, 24, 25, 27, 126
T'ang Shao-i, 80
T'ao Ch'eng-chang, 26, 52, 104
Tchitcherin (Georgi Chicherin), 88
Teng K'eng, 34, 68
Teng Tse-ju, 82, 96
Teng Yen-ta, 82, 88, 95
Ting Ching-liang, 129, 138
Tong, Hollington K., 4, 17, 111, 119, 124
Training Board of Kwangtung Army Headquarters, 98
Trotsky, 88
Ts'ao K'un, 74
Tseng Kuo-fan, 16, 37, 38, 52, 56, 57, 58-59, 104, 135
Tseng Yüan-fu, 38
Tsu Tsung-t'ang, 58
Tsou Lu, 82, 84, 134; administrative ability questioned, 95
Tsou Jung, 20, 52
Tuan Ch'i-jui, 74
T'ung-meng-hui, 19, 118, 125; membership roster, 123
Wang Ching-wei, 24, 32, 47, 50, 70, 71, 74, 75, 76, 77, 81, 82, 84, 85, 88, 89, 90, 95, 105, 135, 145, 146, 150, 155, 156; by nature a compromiser, 97
Wang Po-ling, 95
Wang Teng-yün, 88
Wang Yang-ming, 56
Wei Pang-p'ing, 145

Whampoa Military Academy, 1, 90, 94, 98, 99-100,
    106; party army, 88, 99; Soviet grant to, 152;
    Preparatory Committee, 91-92, 95; funding, 95-
    96; foundation of Chiang's personal power, 96,
    99, 100-01; and Soviet-inspired organization,
    98
Wu Chung-hsin, 130, 138
Wu P'ei-fu, 50; as external enemy, 74
Wu T'ing-fang, 145
Yang Hsi-chi, 146
Yang Hsi-min, 82, 155
Yang Hsi-yen, 96
Yang Hu, 29, 130, 131, 146
Yang Shu-k'an, 50, 82, 84, 85, 86, 96, 138, 146;
    too lazy, 51, 90; governor of Kwangtung, 89-90,
    91, 94, 154
Yao Tsung-yüan, 11
Yen Hsi-shan, 1
Yen-t'ai Naval Academy, 31
Yo Fei, 120
Yü Chien-kuang, 129, 138
Yü Fei-p'eng, 95
Yü Yu-jen, 123
Yüan Shih-k'ai, 15, 27, 30

216

PUBLICATIONS OF THE EAST ASIAN INSTITUTE

STUDIES

The Ladder of Success in Imperial China, by Ping-ti Ho. New York: Columbia University Press, 1962.

The Chinese Inflation, 1937-1949, by Shun-hsin Chou. New York: Columbia University Press, 1963.

Reformer in Modern China: Chang Chien, 1853-1926, by Samuel Chu. New York: Columbia University Press, 1965.

Research in Japanese Sources: A Guide, by Herschel Webb with the assistance of Marleigh Ryan. New York: Columbia University Press, 1965.

Society and Education in Japan, by Herbert Passin. New York: Bureau of Publications, Teachers College, Columbia University, 1965.

Agricultural Production and Economic Development in Japan, 1873-1922, by James I. Nakamura. Princeton: Princeton University Press, 1966.

Japan's First Modern Novel: Ukigumo of Futabatei Shimei, by Marleigh Ryan. New York: Columbia University Press, 1967.

The Korean Communist Movement, 1918-1948, by Dae-Sook Suh. Princeton: Princeton University Press, 1967.

The First Vietnam Crisis, by Melvin Gurtov. New York: Columbia University Press, 1967. Paperback edition, 1968.

Cadres, Bureaucracy, and Political Power in Communist China, by A. Doak Barnett. New York: Columbia University Press, 1967.

The Japanese Imperial Institution in the Tokugawa Period, by Herschel Webb. New York: Columbia University Press, 1968.

Higher Education and Business Recruitment in Japan, by Koya Azumi. New York: Teachers College Press, Columbia University, 1969.

The Communists and Chinese Peasant Rebellion: A Study in the Rewriting of Chinese History, by James P. Harrison, Jr. New York: Atheneum Publishers, 1969.

How the Conservatives Rule Japan, by Nathaniel B. Thayer. Princeton: Princeton University Press, 1969.

Aspects of Chinese Education, edited by C.T. Hu. New York: Teachers College Press, Columbia University, 1969.

Economic Development and the Labor Market in Japan, by Koji Taira. New York: Columbia University Press, 1970.

The Japanese Oligarchy and the Russo-Japanese War, by Shumpei Okamoto. New York: Columbia University Press, 1970.

Japanese Education: A Bibliography of Materials in the English Language, by Herbert Passin. New York: Teachers College Press, Columbia University, 1970.

Documents of Korean Communism, 1918-1948, by Dae-Sook Suh. Princeton: Princeton University Press, 1970.

Japan's Postwar Defense Policy, 1947-1968, by Martin E. Weinstein. New York: Columbia University Press, 1971.

Election Campaigning Japanese Style, by Gerald L. Curtis. New York: Columbia University Press, 1971.

China and Russia: The "Great Game," by O. Edmund Clubb. New York: Columbia University Press, 1971.

Imperial Restoration in Medieval Japan, by H. Paul Varley. New York: Columbia University Press, 1971.

Money and Monetary Policy in Communist China during the First Five Year Plan, by Katharine H. Hsiao. New York: Columbia University Press, forthcoming.

Law and Policy in China's Foreign Relations, by
James C. Hsiung. New York: Columbia University
Press, forthcoming.
Research Guide to Japan's Foreign Policy, 1868-1941,
edited by James W. Morley. New York: Columbia
University Press, forthcoming.
Theory and Practice in Chinese District Administra-
tion, by John R. Watt. New York: Columbia Uni-
versity Press, forthcoming.

RESEARCH AIDS

Sino-Japanese Relations, 1862-1927: A Checklist of
the Chinese Foreign Ministry Archives, compiled
by Kuo Ting-yee and edited by James W. Morley.
New York: East Asian Institute, Columbia Univer-
sity, 1965.
The Research Activities of the South Manchurian
Railway Company, 1907-1945: A History and Bib-
liography, by John Young. New York: East Asian
Institute, Columbia University, 1966.
Chinese Law Past and Present: A Bibliography of
Enactments and Commentaries in English Text,
compiled and edited by Fu-shun Lin. New York:
East Asian Institute, Columbia University, 1966.
A Bibliography of Secondary English Language Liter-
ature on Contemporary Chinese Politics, by
Michel C. Oksenberg with Nancy Bateman and James
B. Anderson. New York: East Asian Institute,
Columbia University, 1970.
A Guide to British Foreign Office: Confidential
Print: China, 1848-1922. Microfilm F.O. 405, by
Carol Reynolds. New York: East Asian Institute,
Columbia University, 1970.

OCCASIONAL PAPERS

Historians and American Far Eastern Policy, compiled by Dorothy Borg. New York: East Asian
Institute, Columbia University, 1966.

*Provincial Party Personnel in Mainland China,
1956-1966*, by Frederick C. Teiwes. New York:
East Asian Institute, Columbia University,
1967.

*Reality and Illusion: The Hidden Crisis Between
Japan and the U.S.S.R., 1932-1934*, by Ikuhiko
Hata. New York: East Asian Institute, Columbia
University, 1967.

Imperial Japan and Asia: A Reassessment, compiled
by Grant K. Goodman. New York: East Asian Institute, Columbia University, 1967.

American Presurrender Planning for Postwar Japan,
by Hugh Borton. New York: East Asian Institute,
Columbia University, 1967.

The Legacy of the Occupation--Japan, by Herbert
Passin. New York: East Asian Institute, Columbia University, 1968.

Taiwan: Studies in Chinese Local History, edited by
Leonard H.D. Gordon. New York: Columbia University Press, 1970.

The Introduction of Socialism into China, by Li Yu-
ning. New York: Columbia University Press, 1971.

*The Early Chiang Kai-shek: A Study of His Personal-
ity and Politics, 1887-1924*, by Pichon P.Y. Loh.
New York: Columbia University Press, 1971.

REPRINTS

The Communist Movement in China, by Ch'en Kung-po,
edited with an Introduction by C. Martin Wilbur.
New York: Octagon Books, 1966.

*American Policy and the Chinese Revolution, 1925-
1928*, by Dorothy Borg. New York: Octagon Books,
1968.

The Fabric of Chinese Society, by Morton H. Fried.
New York: Octagon Books, 1970.